# PLEASURABLE INSTRUCTION

Thomas Rowlandson's drawing, "Doctor Syntax Reading His Tour," plate 23 in William Combe's *Tour of Doctor Syntax, in Search of the Picturesque* (London, [1812]).

# PLEASURABLE INSTRUCTION

## Form and Convention in Eighteenth-Century Travel Literature

By CHARLES L. BATTEN, JR.

University of California Press, Berkeley, Los Angeles, London

University of California Press
Berkeley and Los Angeles, California

University of California Press, Ltd.
London, England

1 2 3 4 5 6 7 8 9 0

Printed in the United States of America

For Anne and Kit

# CONTENTS

# CONTENTS

# PREFACE

Writing in the 1780s, Count Leopold Berchtold claimed that a traveler must "before he sets out for any place, have an accurate description of the curiosities of the road that leads to it." The same may be said of the reader of this book, who undoubtedly wants some idea not only of the purpose of the trip on which I take him but also of the rareties he will encounter along the way.

Simply stated, the goal of this book is a generic description of one of the most popular literary forms of the eighteenth century, the nonfiction travel account. But in order to reach this objective, I must lead my reader on a road that, though direct, needs several signposts along the way. After an introductory discussion of the importance and popularity of eighteenth-century nonfiction travel literature together with the need for a definition of its form and conventions, I suggest, in chapter one, the general outlines of what the century called "voyages and travels." To do this, I focus first on Addison's *Remarks on Several Parts of Italy* (1705), a convenient *terminus a quo* because of its publication date, its widespread influence, and its changing reputation during the century. I then use Smollett's *Expedition of Humphry Clinker* (1771) and *Travels through France and Italy* (1766) to distinguish generically between fictional and nonfictional travels, and Horace's famous dictum concerning pleasure and instruction to indicate the manner in which the eighteenth century saw travels as being genuinely "literary." All this leads to a description at the end of chapter one of the general form employed by travel writers during the century, showing how they blended accounts of their own experiences with descriptions of the countries they visited. Chapters two and three define the basic conventions used by travelers to narrate experiences and to describe geographical regions, showing how these conventions significantly changed toward the end of the century and suggesting some of the artistic problems and literary influences which may have caused these developments. The Conclusion then recommends the ways in which eighteenth-century travel accounts should and should not be interpreted by readers, many of whom in the past have tried to see the century's travelers primarily as precursors of a new romantic sensibility.

"*Is This Trip Necessary?*" The sign greeted many a traveler during World War II, and it might easily be modified to read "*Is This Book Necessary?*" for many an author today. My answer to the latter question is yes, though I will leave it up to my readers to decide if I have taken the proper and profitable route. Nonfiction travel accounts, while certainly the most common of all eighteenth-century voyages and travels, have scarcely enjoyed the kind of critical attention lavished on their fictional cousins, the imaginary voyage and the travel lie. Philip Babcock Gove's *Imaginary Voyage in Prose Fiction* (1941) and Percy G. Adams's *Travelers and Travel Liars* (1962) have contributed greatly to our understanding of eighteenth-century literature and culture, but each work ignores the formal characteristics of nonfiction travel literature. The same can be said about other studies like Hans-Joachim Possin's *Reisen und Literatur* (1972) and the numerous descriptions of the grand tour published over the last century. Even the major bibliographers of travel literature have compiled their lists without defining either what they or the eighteenth century considered to be a travel account. *Pleasurable Instruction* consequently attempts to supply an obvious need, the definition and description of what the London *Chronicle* called the most "agreeable and enchanting" of all "species of literary composition."

"*How could you journey throughout France without seeing Chartres?*" Virtually every traveler encountering such a greeting upon returning home must answer friends with "*There simply wasn't time to see everything*" or "*Chartres just wasn't in my path.*" I fear I must plead along similar lines when asked why I have failed to discuss at length some favorite work like Baron de Lahontan's *New Voyages to North-America* (1703) or Southey's *Letters Written during a Short*

*Residence in Spain and Portugal* (1797). A good deal of selectivity is necessary when dealing with the massive publications of travel accounts which the eighteenth century witnessed. For this reason I concentrate upon the century's most popular voyages and travels together with those that make critical comments about form or convention and those that incited the most spirited praise or distaste among reviewers. While travel literature was a truly international genre during the century, I have largely confined myself to English accounts and to those that were translated into English. (In the latter case, I cite the English title in my text, followed in parenthesis by the original date of publication and the date of the English translation.) Though some of the travel accounts I discuss reach into the remoter regions of the earth, a large portion of them deal with Great Britain and the Continent. The reason for this is simple: the most popular and the most influential travelers, more frequently than not, describe places relatively near to home. The selectivity in this work should not, however, harm its conclusions since the century was quite unanimous in its attitudes toward the proper form of travel literature whether it described the wilds of Canada or the refinements of Paris.

While this book's errors are all mine, its virtues frequently result from the people who helped me along the way. Gratitude must first of all go to my colleague, Gordon L. Kipling, who read more versions of my manuscript than I would like to remember. His continued assistance and friendship kept me from straying into the wrong paths, and for this he deserves to be called *il miglior fabbro*. Additional thanks go to Gwin J. Kolb and Arthur Friedman, who started me on this study, and to Anne and Kit Batten, who helped me finish it. My footnotes would still be in a shoebox were it not for the diligence of James F. McCloskey, and my manuscript would still be illegible were it not for the patience of Jeanette Gilkison. Anne Cummings slaved patiently over a Xerox machine for me, while Cheryl F. Giuliano and Udo Strutynski of the University of California Press gave me the kind of help one would expect only from friends. Research for this book was completed with the assistance of a Regents Faculty Fellowship and grants from the UCLA Research Committee. The staffs of the UCLA Research Library, the William Andrews Clark Memorial Library, the Henry E. Huntington Library, the University of Chicago Library, and the Newberry Library deserve the kind of personal thanks that I cannot give them here. Finally, my gratitude goes to the editors of *Genre* for allowing me to reprint revised excerpts of my article, "*Humphry Clinker* and Eighteenth-Century Travel Literature," as part of chapter one.

If you think I impose too great a task on your inquisitive traveller, my next advice is, That he stay at home: read *Europe* in the mirror of his own country, which but too eagerly reflects and flatters every state that dances before its surface; and, for the rest, take up with the best information he can get from the books and narratives of the best voyagers.

—"Mr. Locke" speaking in Bishop Richard Hurd's *On the Uses of Foreign Travel* (1763)

# INTRODUCTION

One of the most distinguishing features in the literary history of our age and country, is the passion of the public for voyages and travels.
— English Editor, Moritz's *Travels* (1795)

"There are no books which I more delight in than in travels," confessed Joseph Addison writing for the *Tatler* in 1710. Although Englishmen had been describing their voyages and journeys for many years, the eighteenth century—ushered in with works like Addison's own *Remarks on Italy*—witnessed a new era in which non-fiction travel literature achieved an unparalleled popularity. Praised by readers and reviewers in terms that ring hyperbolic in twentieth-century ears, these accounts won a readership second only to novels by the end of the century.[1] "Of all the various productions of the press," writes Ralph Griffiths in the *Monthly Review* for March 1768, "none are so eagerly received by us Reviewers, and other people who stay at home and mind our business, as the writings of travellers." Fellow reviewers echo these sentiments, claiming that voyages and travels are "universally acceptable" and always worthy of "a favourable reception from the public."[2] Naturalists, geographers, and moral philosophers eagerly awaited new travels as they came from the press, and even young women, like Jane Austen's romance-addicted heroine, had to admit that they did not "dislike" them. Descriptions from travel accounts served as some of the most powerful ammunition in the century's theological battles over the pagan gods, natural religion, and human nature.[3] Public libraries found it difficult to stock such works as Patrick Brydone's *Tour through Sicily and Malta* (1773), which quickly went through numerous London

1

and Dublin editions, and John Hawkesworth's *Account of the Voyages...in the Southern Hemisphere* (1773), for which its editor earned the astonishing sum of £6,000.[4] Moreover, travel accounts found honored places on the shelves of Addison, Locke, Johnson, Hume, Gibbon, and Jefferson, influencing their ideas about geography, science, and human nature.[5] There can be small wonder at Robert Gray's observation toward the end of the century that "no taste" prevails more "than that for books of travels," to which William Mavor added, "of all studies, not absolutely necessary" to man's well-being, "none are more cherished."[6]

This popularity in part resulted from the economic and technological gains that made travel possible for increased numbers of the reading public during the eighteenth century. No longer did the sojourner in foreign parts have to face the extreme physical hardships mentioned in Paul Hentzner's *Itinerarium* (1611) or Thomas Coryate's *Crudities* (1611). Especially in France, roads and carriages improved phenomenally during the century. Accommodations and food on the Continent, though often complained of, were at least available on the most frequently traveled routes. Even the dizzying trip over the Alps had become almost comfortable with the introduction of professional guides. Relative military calm also helped open the doors to an influx of "Milords," and some 40,000 of them, according to Walpole, passed through Calais during the twenty-four months after the Peace of 1763. In the following decade, so James Rutledge asserts, Parisian society had the opportunity to threaten the morals of at least three thousand Englishmen at any given time.[7] No longer was the Continental *giro* restricted to the wealthy few with their entourage of baggage and servants. Increasingly the middle class enjoyed this polite recreation, especially with the advent of the pedestrian tour toward the end of the century. The further reaches of the globe also opened up to more travelers. Africa, India, the Spice Islands, and the Americas—places previously visited mainly by ships' captains, adventurers, and explorers—now with growing frequency inspired travel descriptions from relatively new classes of people: natural philosophers, minor employees of the trading companies, seamen on merchant and military ships, and even an occasional woman. As a consequence, travel literature did not solely provide a window on the world for those Englishmen who stayed at home. By developing a largely practical appeal, it helped some readers decide where to go and what to see, it assisted them in the everyday problems of selecting suitable lodging, food, and transportation, and it aided their lagging memories once they returned home.

But the increase in travel during the eighteenth century scarcely explains the extraordinary popularity of travel literature. After all, people in the twentieth century travel more frequently than they did in the eighteenth, but today we either ignore travel accounts or dismiss them as artistically unimportant. The eighteenth century, however, saw the writing of a travel account as an important undertaking for the well-educated man or woman who, having made a trip, wished to convey in an artistically pleasing fashion the information he had gleaned. Thus Richardson appropriately chooses this fashionable enterprise as a way of cementing the relationship between Lovelace, who has just returned from the grand tour, and Clarissa, who directs the writing down of his observations and reflections. During the century, travel literature attracted the most important writers of the day, from Addison and Defoe to Fielding, Smollett, Boswell, and Johnson. Clearly aware of the literary demands of their age, they wrote in a firmly defined tradition, sometimes influencing subtle changes in it. Most of these authors commented upon the travel accounts written by their predecessors and contemporaries, sharply criticizing those that departed from tradition. Their enthusiasm for this genre made the travel account a respected literary form that conveyed pleasant instruction to an age thirsty for information about foreign countries as well as their own homeland.

Twentieth-century studies have almost uniformly ignored the literary value and distinctive generic characteristics of eighteenth-century nonfiction travel literature. Instead, most treatments of the travel book are social histories, like Rosamond Bayne-Powell's *Travellers in Eighteenth-Century England* (1951), which attempt to determine what the traveler "saw . . . how he travelled and was entertained, whether he liked his hosts, and what they thought of him, and his various reactions to what he saw and experienced."[8] Fre-

quently, such information serves to demonstrate the rise of romanti-
cism. George B. Parks thus typically finds the increase of natural
descriptions in travel books an indicator of a change in Western civilization's aesthetic appreciation for the beauties of nature.[9]

But these sociohistorical studies face a methodological problem
that renders their findings ambiguous at best and misleading at
worst. By ignoring the literary conventions that govern what an
author says, they assume that these accounts display the immediate,
personal experiences of travelers, and that these travelers in turn
reflect the tastes of the century in general. In fact, however, convention often governs a travel writer's actions and descriptions. He
might find himself in a particular spot not because he personally
wished to visit it, but because he had to write about it in order to
give a comprehensive or novel or balanced picture of a foreign country.[10] In addition, technical problems may stop a traveler from describing a site that genuinely moves him. Attempting to picture the
Temple of Anaitis, for example, Boswell threw up his hands in despair when searching for "such particulars as might give some idea
of it, and of the surrounding scenery." Because of the "great difficulty of describing visible objects," Boswell ultimately found his
account so unsatisfactory that he tore it up. It will not do, therefore,
to complain that "Boswell could journey in Switzerland, Italy, and
Corsica in the 1760's with not the slightest attention to nature."[11]
Absence of a particular kind of description in a travel book scarcely
proves that its author was inattentive or unappreciative.

Clearly, then, some definition of travel literature is necessary. But
a work like Addison's *Remarks on Italy* differs fundamentally from
Thomas Coryate's *Crudities,* published some 84 years earlier, and
Alexander Kinglake's *Eöthen,* published almost 140 years later: the
Spectator's account specifically lacks Coryate's chatty discourse on
the one hand and Kinglake's vivid descriptions on the other. Indeed,
no one familiar with eighteenth-century voyages and travels would
agree with Henri M. Peyre's recent claim that in travel literature,
"the traveller himself has always counted for more than the places
he visited." So little formal similarity exists between the accounts
written by travelers of different centuries that any general definition
of them, according to F. A. Kirkpatrick, would be difficult.[12] Never-

theless, eighteenth-century authors persistently thought of travel literature as a new kind of development, possessing characteristics
never before seen in the accounts of travelers. As Nathaniel Wraxall
indicates in his *Cursory Remarks* (1775), "the age of imposition on
one side, and of credulity on the other seems now to be past."
"Truth and sound knowledge" can serve as the subjects of travel literature "where formerly they scarce ever intruded."[13] Indeed, eighteenth-century travel literature operates as a corrective, in the words
of the *Critical Review,* for those works written from the "end of the
fourth to the conclusion of the last century" in which authors were
either "of a romantic turn" or simply "satisfied with appearances."
Those earlier romantic writers mixed fact with fiction, exposing the
English public to outrageous lies dealing with what Shaftesbury
called "the most unnatural and monstrous" things.[14] Many of these
travel books, as a consequence, bear striking similarities to Elizabethan romances, sharing not only a general lack of realism but also
"much superficial machinery...the journeys, the shipwrecks, the
narrow escapes, the captivities, the exotic settings, peoples, and
manners." Hills touching heaven, like Anthropophagi and men with
heads beneath their shoulders, had long been commonplaces in
travel accounts by the time Othello seduced Desdemona with his
"travel's history," and headless men together with mermaids served
as standard fare for Renaissance travelers who, according to Bishop
Hall in 1598, liked to tickle the ears of brainsick youths.[15] Authentic
travel books, on the contrary, were often written by travelers who,
lacking "sound knowledge," satisfied themselves simply with appearances. Such accounts tended to be superficial and written in an
inelegant manner; attacking them, Shaftesbury remarked that their
"facts unably related, though with the greatest sincerity and good
faith, may prove the worst sort of deceit." The authors of these
works seem largely to have been men "who had received no more
than a grammar school education and who wrote little besides the
accounts of their voyages." Since "most of the narratives were written for the practical purpose of providing a record of a voyage,"
they scarcely can be called "literary."[16]

Rebelling against its Renaissance ancestors, the eighteenth-century travel account achieved a generic blending of factual informa-

tion and literary art. A "thirst for knowledge" now joined a lust for gold in motivating the typical traveler in his search through foreign lands,[17] and this traveler could now return home with the notes for an entertaining and instructive travel account, a prize of more value to some than the rarest gem. Our modern dissociation of science and belles lettres had not as yet occurred in this age in which the educated reader could still be a "universal man" mastering many subjects. Because of its wide readership and influential practition-ers, travel literature of the eighteenth century provides an important key to the intellectual, cultural, and literary history of the English people. But in the hands of scholars who do not understand its generic conventions, it can easily be misinterpreted in order to prove all kinds of misleading generalizations about individual works or about literary trends. For instance, one critic of Johnson's *Journey to the Western Islands of Scotland* (1775) expresses a feeling that is probably quite pervasive in the twentieth century: "To the reader looking for anecdotes, Johnson is disappointing." Then, in order to rescue Johnson's reputation, he explains how three themes are artis-tically "interwoven, contrasted, counterpointed, and modulated" in *A Journey.* Another critic traces what he calls the "theme of travel" through such generically dissimilar books as Bunyan's *Pilgrim's Progress,* Addison's *Remarks,* Smollett's *Humphry Clinker,* and Sterne's *Sentimental Journey,* claiming they all belong to a thematic tradition "which could be called the 'moralistic' phase of English travel literature."[18] An eighteenth-century reader, expecting neither anecdotal subject matter nor thematic organization in a travel book, would probably only laugh at such blatant disregard for generic convention.

"If a young man is ambitious to raise a reputation in the world, or to improve in knowledge and wisdom," explains Philostratus in *The Life of Apollonius of Tyana* (c. 200 A.D.), "he should travel into foreign countries."[19] The eighteenth century took this maxim seri-ously, modifying it a bit as factually accurate travel literature be-came ever more popular. While men like Addison clearly set out on their journeys for the sake of earning reputations, others could stay at home, where they might glean knowledge and wisdom by reading the voyages and travels of their more adventurous and wealthy fellows. The travel account thus opened up the world to the man who for one reason or another could not visit places like the Holy Land, America, or even the shores of the Mediterranean. Dr. Johnson himself belonged to the latter group; though he always felt an inferiority for not having seen Italy, and though he was known to express late in life the improbable desire to visit the Great Wall of China, he largely made up for these deficiencies by devouring virtually every travel book published during his mature years.

An old proverb had said: "Travellers must be allowed to tell what Stories they please; 'tis better to believe what [the traveler] saith than to go and seek out the Truth of it."[20] But the eighteenth century was beginning to put the lie to this, frequently substituting honest descriptions for the fabulous narratives of previous travelers. Like Cowper in *The Task* (1785), many an Englishman could now muse with enjoyment upon a traveler's factually accurate tale:

> He travels and expatiates, as the bee
> From flow'r to flow'r, so he from land to land;
> The manners, customs, policy of all
> Pay contribution to the store he gleans;
> He sucks intelligence in ev'ry clime,
> And spreads the honey of his deep research
> At his return—a rich repast for me.
> He travels, and I too. I tread his deck,
> Ascend his topmast, through his peering eyes
> Discover countries, with a kindred heart
> Suffer his woes, and share in his escapes;
> While fancy, like the finger of a clock,
> Runs the great circuit, and is still at home.
> [IV, 107-119]

For the eighteenth century, then, the travel writer was first of all a researcher, "sucking" intelligence from different geographical regions. The English editor of Sparrman's *Voyage to the Cape of Good Hope* (Swedish 1783; English 1785) would have it that "every authentic and well-written book of voyages and travels is, in fact, a treatise of experimental philosophy."[21] Travel books, however, were not merely treatises, since they also provided an imaginative experience for the reader who happened to have a "kindred heart." They conveyed, in short, the kind of mimetic entertainment more often associated with narrative literature than with merely philosophical studies. Thus in an age anxious to learn about the world in which it lived, the travel account joined pleasure with instruction in what became, perhaps, one of the most characteristic forms of the century.

# I

## TOWARD A DEFINITION OF EIGHTEENTH-CENTURY NONFICTION TRAVEL LITERATURE

---

*I'll make a* TOUR—*and then I'll* WRITE IT.
    —Combe, *Tour of Dr. Syntax in Search of the Picturesque* (1812)

### *Addison's* Remarks on Italy *and Its Readers*

In a century during which many men and women composed travel accounts and even more undertook journeys, Joseph Addison often stood out among his contemporaries as a model writer if not a totally typical traveler. His grand tour of Europe began inauspiciously in the summer of 1699 with a misplaced step that almost drowned him in the English Channel at Calais. What followed was a series of "Bruises upon Land, lame post-horses by Day and hard Beds at night," all suffered for the sake of gaining an experience that would qualify him for a diplomatic career. The grand tour had long been an established ritual for England's gentlemen by the time Addison retreated to Blois in order to learn French. But unlike the average English gentleman, who undertook the grand tour between the ages of sixteen and twenty-one, Addison at twenty-seven knew how to take best advantage of his travels. His experiences might easily have served to support Locke's theories concerning the educational function of travel. Well past the "Season to get Foreign Languages," Addison, as Locke predicted, had great trouble mastering French. But the maturity that tied his tongue admirably suited him to make observations of foreign countries which would "be of use to him

9

after his return" to England, thus distinguishing him from the
majority of adolescent travelers who merely gained "an admiration
of the worst and vainest Practices they met with abroad."[1]

Addison's tumble into the Channel aptly foreshadowed his initial
failure to achieve the official goal of his continental travels. Back in
England, the death of William III turned Addison's political friends
out of power and defeated his hopes of securing an appointment as a
royal secretary to Prince Eugene of Savoy. Indeed, political prefer-
ment eluded Addison until November of 1704, when he succeeded
Locke as a Commissioner of Appeal in Excise. But while Addison's
travels contributed little directly to his diplomatic career, the record
of his observations during the grand tour helped establish his fame
as an author. Appearing in November of 1705, his *Remarks on Several Parts of Italy, &c.* gradually became the one work any Englishman interested in Italy felt obliged to consult.

The popularity and influence of these observations can scarcely
be overstated. In addition to printings in his collected works, *Remarks on Italy* went through at least thirteen separate editions during the eighteenth century, appearing also in French and Dutch
translations.[2] By the time it was epitomized in such frequently reprinted collections as *The World Displayed* (1760-1761) and William Mavor's *Historical Account of the Most Celebrated Voyages*
(1796-1797), the book had become an ackowledged contemporary
classic.[3] Shortly after its initial publication, Jean Le Clerc read it on
the Continent with "beaucoup de plaisir," and the *Journal des Sçavans* declared it "un Livre tres-agréable." John Durant Breval, who
traveled to Italy some twenty years after Addison, felt that no traveler had written "Memoirs in our Tongue that can be of half the
Service" as *Remarks on Italy.* And no less an author than Henry
Fielding praised Addison as one of the few travelers able to offer his
readers something more than dullness.[4]

Thanks to such an enthusiastic reception, *Remarks on Italy*
rapidly became a standard *vade mecum* for the Englishman on his
grand tour. Typical of many eighteenth-century travelers, James
Boswell went to the Continent with a copy of *Remarks on Italy*
tucked away in his luggage, ready to read it "with high relish" once
he crossed Addison's path. Encountering his mentor's route for the

first time in Soleure, Boswell expresses almost fawning praise for the paltry, one-paragraph description of this town in *Remarks on Italy:* "Does not the Spectator's having been here give a value to it. It is mighty agreeable to read Mr. Addison's observations and then look at what he has described." Boswell's enthusiasm for Addison's *Remarks* was so great that he planned to "enrich" his journal by systematically comparing the Italy he saw with the Italy Addison had seen some sixty years earlier. While Boswell never followed through with these plans, the influence of *Remarks on Italy* on his work can scarcely be doubted. Upon arriving at Milan, for instance, Boswell found himself repeating "Et Mediolani mira omnia, copia rerum," the opening line of Ausonius's description of Milan which Addison quotes in his travel book. While there, Boswell went to the cathedral but refused to say much about the statues of Saint Bartholomew and the shrine of Charles Borromeo, since they had been "enough described by others" — most notably Addison. Boswell even performed an acoustical experiment that his predecessor had undertaken. Having walked to a deserted palace about a league from Milan, Boswell fired a pistol and counted fifty-eight echoes; the same experiment had produced for Addison only fifty-six. Finally, Boswell followed Addison's steps to Milan's Ambrosian Library, where he corrected his mentor's statement that the library owned a portrait of only one Englishman, Bishop Fisher. Boswell surely exaggerated when he claimed that "the least expression" in *Remarks on Italy* was as valuable as "the least bits of the precious diamond." Nevertheless, a host of other eighteenth-century travelers would have agreed with him in calling Addison's book "my Classic while I travel in Italy."[5]

While casual references to *Remarks on Italy* creep into the letters and private journals of such travelers as James Boswell, Lady Mary Wortley Montagu, Horace Walpole, and Edward Gibbon,[6] the real influence of Addison's travel book most clearly comes to light in the various accounts published by travelers who followed him on the grand tour. From Breval's *Remarks on Several Parts of Europe* (1726) — its title conspicuously modeled after that of Addison's *Remarks* — to Mrs. Piozzi's *Observations and Reflections* (1789), virtually every eighteenth-century travel description of Italy bears witness to its author's familiarity with Addison's work. Travel writers like

Keyssler, Moore, Sharp, and Smollett make numerous references to
Addison, sometimes praising him, often refusing to describe places
already treated by him, and most frequently correcting his mistaken
observations and opinions.[7] Generations of England's gentlemen
must have traveled through Italy with copies of *Remarks on Italy,* if
not in their hands, at least hidden in convenient pockets. At the beginning of the nineteenth century, John Chetwode Eustace commented that *Remarks on Italy* was still the generally recommended
guide for Englishmen on the grand tour, and as late as 1952, Paul
Franklin Kirby pointed out that Addison's book, in spite of its age,
was nevertheless known to the general tourist in Italy.[8] *Remarks on
Italy* exerted wide influence on what the eighteenth-century traveler
saw and described, thus affecting the artistic and literary tastes not
only of the man who went on the grand tour but also of the man who
stayed at home. Indeed, Addison's *Remarks* even influenced the
poetry of Joseph Warton and Alexander Pope, neither of whom ever
visited the classical sites of Italy.[9]

Despite its popularity, *Remarks on Italy* did not escape its share
of unfavorable criticism. To be sure, some of its eighteenth-century
detractors attacked it simply because its author was a Whig, others
because he was big game—one of the foremost authors of his day.
But other readers found fault with Addison's *Remarks* on literary
grounds, using criteria that conveniently define the specific generic
characteristics of eighteenth-century travel literature. The first such
sustained attack, *A Table of All the Accurate Remarks and New
Discoveries, in . . . Mr. Addison's Book of Travels* (1706), censures
Addison on two crucial grounds: his handling of the narrative of his
experiences and, more significantly, his reliance on passages from
the classics to describe the countries through which he traveled. By
attacking Addison's narrative and descriptive techniques, *A Table*
thus points to the major artistic concerns of the eighteenth-century
writer and reader of travel literature.

*A Table* first of all singles out for censure several passages like the
following that probably strike the twentieth-century reader as being
quite appropriate in modern travel literature:

> The Author had the good Luck to be at *Florence* when there
> was an Opera Acted, which was the 8th he had seen in *Italy.*

> The Author mistook Linnen on the Ground for a Lake.
> The Author's Merchants advis'd him not to venture himself
> in the Duke of *Bavaria*'s Country.[10]

In each of these statements, Addison relates feelings and experiences: that he felt fortunate to attend an opera, that he made a mistake in what he saw, that he received certain advice from his merchants. But in these few instances Addison violates what we shall see is a clearly defined convention of eighteenth-century travel literature: a travel writer must not talk about himself.

Nineteenth- and twentieth-century readers have frequently misunderstood this convention, usually expecting to find in *Remarks on Italy* considerably more anecdotal and autobiographical material than would have been admissible in an eighteenth-century travel account, especially one written by a relative unknown in his early thirties. Thomas Babington Macaulay falls into this critical trap when complaining of Addison's failure to treat "politics and scandal, speculations on the projects of Victor Amadeus, and anecdotes about the jollities of convents and the amours of cardinals and nuns." By the time Macaulay wrote these words, readers of travel books had frequently come to expect a subject matter that now featured chatty and rather trivial information. Indeed, Macaulay's mistitling of Addison's work as a *Narrative of His Travels in Italy* reveals a fundamental misconception. Scarcely an appropriate title for an eighteenth-century travel book containing very little narrative material, it would serve well for a nineteenth-century work like Alexander Kinglake's *Eöthen,* which extensively narrates its author's experiences. Similarly, William Spalding's article on Addison, which appeared in the *Encyclopaedia Britannica* from the mid-nineteenth through the early twentieth century, depreciates *Remarks on Italy* for lacking "altogether the interest of personal narrative," a quality that scarcely distinguishes Addison's book from most other eighteenth-century travel accounts. In an even more misleading fashion, Edmund Gosse explains away the frigid, impersonal nature of Addison's *Remarks* by supposing that "the colourless purity of Addison's style at this period" did not lend itself to descriptions. In the same vein, Bonamy Dobrée thinks *Remarks on Italy* lacks "individual touches" though it is "not quite so anonymously

colourless as most guide-books are." Such damning with faint praise
leads Dobrée almost paradoxically to conclude that *Remarks on
Italy*, while "in no way contemptible," nevertheless has "small literary worth."[11] This twentieth-century judgment helps perpetuate
nineteenth-century misconceptions of eighteenth-century travel literature.    But above all, Addison's staggering use of classical quotations—some 141 in total—caused him to suffer the abuse and sometimes the laughter of readers from the eighteenth century to the
present.[12] *A Table*, for example, sarcastically points out that unlike
other travelers, Addison does not inquire into "*the Constitutions,
the Laws, the Policies, the Leagues, the Commerce, and Genius of
those Countries and Cities*" through which he passed. Rather than
undertaking such so-called idle investigations, Addison furnishes
important information, namely, "The ends of Verse / And sayings of
Philosophers."[13] Similar attacks had appeared from the pens of
others by the time Horace Walpole parodied *Remarks on Italy* in a
delightfully silly letter to Thomas Gray (1735) and Laurence Sterne
pictured in Volume VII of *Tristram Shandy* "the great *Addison*"
writing his travels with a "satchel of school-books hanging from his
a[rse] and galling his beast's crupper at every stroke."[14]

   But by using these numerous classical quotations, Addison is able
to follow two conventional demands made of eighteenth-century
travel accounts. These demands, which perhaps helped mold the
aesthetic principles he lays forth in "The Pleasures of the Imagination" in the *Spectator*, lead the traveler to include descriptions that
are novel in content and clear in the manner in which they portray
the country. Addison confesses as much in his Preface, where he explains: "*As I have taken notice of several Places and Antiquities that
no body else has spoken of, so, I think, I have mentioned but few
things in common with others, that are not either set in a new light,
or accompanied with different reflections.*" Having examined the
accounts of his predecessors, he concluded that room existed for yet
another description of Italy so long as it was novel in approach. To
do this, Addison set about to collect "*passages of the ancient Poets*"
which would enable him to compare the "*natural face*" of Italy with
the "*Landskips*" described by classical authors. But he did not
intend his travel account to be a purely pedantic exercise, since its
numerous classical quotations were meant to convey "*some Image*"
of the places he described.

However important these generic demands might have been to writers like Addison, they have caused serious problems for those modern readers who have attempted to deal with eighteenth-century travel accounts as if they were unrestrained autobiographies. Thus, while Bonamy Dobrée correctly points out that Addison was "interested in the antiquities" of Italy "for what they remind[ed] him of in Virgil, Ovid, Silius Italicus, or whoever," he clearly misses the mark when he infers from *Remarks on Italy* that Addison was "not much interested in people" and that he showed only a "languid interest in the sights to be seen."[15] Though Addison's frequent quotations certainly reflect a lifelong passion for the classics, his silence concerning certain other subjects scarcely reflects a lack of interest in them. No one could possibly say that Addison disliked eating and sleeping simply because, like most other eighteenth-century travelers, he does not mention food and lodging. Generic convention, not personal taste, dictates to a great extent what a traveler says. Thus Francis Watt can look in vain through John Durant Breval's travel accounts for the famous story, alluded to in Pope's *Dunciad* (1742-1743), of Breval's escapade with a nun who had been confined against her will in a convent at Milan.[16] Such a narrative simply would not have been an acceptable subject for a travel account.

The problem of interpreting personal feelings in a travel account becomes even more acute once twentieth-century critics begin attempting to date the origin of "romantic" sensibilities by using Addison's descriptions of mountain scenery. Clarence DeWitt Thorpe, for example, cites Addison's use of Silius Italicus's somewhat appreciative description of the Alps to prove that the traveler aesthetically approved of mountains, while Donald F. Bond implies that Addison's reliance on classical passages argues against it.[17] The Addison who likes mountains is an early "romantic"; the one who dislikes them remains a "classicist." Because of its descriptions, *Remarks on Italy* frequently appears as a central document in this debate, and in some quarters Addison's book earns him a reputation as a "preromantic" among such contenders for the title as Gray, Shaftesbury, Philips, Collins, Thomson, and Dennis.[18]

To some extent, most of these arguments share the basic aesthetic premises of Marjorie Hope Nicolson's *Mountain Gloom and Mountain Glory*. "During the first seventeen centuries of the Christian

era," Nicolson explains, " 'Mountain Gloom' so clouded human eyes
that never for a moment did poets see mountains in the full radiance
to which our eyes have become accustomed." But then suddenly,
"within a century—indeed, within fifty years"—a "Mountain Glory"
first appeared, ultimately shining with "full splendor." This argument of course depends upon the questionable assumption that we,
"like men of every age," "see in Nature what we have been taught to
look for" and "feel what we have been prepared to feel."[19] From this
point of view, Silius Italicus could have experienced no romantic
elation when viewing the Alps. Consequently, since aesthetic appreciations of nature are acquired rather than universal, they can be
explained in terms of the history of ideas.

At least two faulty theories characterize the abuse that eighteenth-
century travel books like *Remarks on Italy* have suffered at the
hands of modern critics. First of all, "the persistent ignoring of the
grand and terrible" is supposed "the most convincing proof for the
prevailing distaste for wild scenery" before the eighteenth century.[20]
But as we have seen, an author's refusal to write about something
scarcely indicates his distaste for it. Established literary convention
often dictates the subjects that eighteenth-century authors discuss
far more surely than does personal taste. Second, certain critics try
to prove that people before the eighteenth century lacked an aesthetic appreciation of mountains by collecting passages in which
writers seem to express hatred or at least distaste for such natural
settings. We typically find that Joshua Poole's *English Parnassus*
(1677 ed.) applies to mountains ugly epithets like "Earth's Dugs,
Risings, Tumors, Blisters...Earth's Warts." But the critic who
amasses these "facts" ignores a fundamental problem in descriptive
literature: how can an author picture mountains for an audience
that has never seen them before? For such readers, these adjectives
and epithets need not necessarily evoke any sense of disgust. (Poole
in any event also suggests that mountains may be described as
"aspiring," "lofty," "stately," "sky-kissing," and "lovely," this last
term appearing twice in his catalog.) Discussing the travel accounts
read by Coleridge, John Livingston Lowes observes that travelers
"like most of us" carry "their known and familiar landscape with
them," catching "glimpses of it through the strangest lights." Poets
and travelers alike must often refer to familiar scenes and objects

4

when describing those that are unfamiliar to their readers. Although not the prettiest metaphor an author might use, "Earth's Warts" serves as an adequate description for people familiar with warts but not with mountains. We must keep this important consideration in mind when reading, for example, John Evelyn's celebrated description of the Alps, which appeared in his eyes to rise "as if nature had ...swept up the rubbish of the Earth in the Alps, to forme and cleare the Plaines of Lombardy." As anyone who has seen the Alps must admit, Evelyn's simile, far from necessarily picturing the mountains in a pejorative light, is above all a vivid description of the geological contrast between the mountains and the flat country that surrounds them. Complaints against Thomas Hobbes's description of the Peak in Darbyshire, which contains what Nicolson considers "one of the worst examples of 'metaphysical' grotesquerie," similarly miss the point. Hobbes does not necessarily display a dislike for mountains when he writes:

> Behind a ruin'd mountain does appear
> Swelling into two parts, which turgent are
> As when we bend our bodies to the ground,
> The buttocks amply sticking out are found.[21]

As a metaphysical conceit, Hobbes's comparison of mountains with buttocks is similar in kind, if not in quality, to Donne's comparison of a woman's loss of virginity with a flea's sucking of blood. Consequently, we dare not solely on the basis of a metaphysical conceit accuse Hobbes of an inability to enjoy mountain scenery any more than we can assert that Donne failed to enjoy seduction simply because he describes it with such a distasteful comparison.

Historians who discuss eighteenth-century travel books frequently forget that they deal with a specific kind of literature. If, as Nicolson asserts, *Remarks on Italy* contains Addison's "emotions recollected in tranquility,"[22] then we might be able to equate his statements with his unfiltered and unadulterated feelings. But *Remarks on Italy* is anything but a spontaneous overflow of emotions, and to read it as a romantic poem is to miss its point entirely. The historian of ideas must first understand the medium through which concepts are expressed before examining and interpreting the concepts them-

selves. When failing to consider the medium, he easily confuses
shifts in ideas with shifts in the rhetorical means of expressing them.
For too long, *Remarks on Italy* has appeared solely as a kind of landmark in the development of a new aesthetic sensibility. Rather, it
must first of all be seen as a stage in experimentation with novel and
vivid descriptions within a conventionally defined framework. We
indeed shall never know the true feelings of a man who, in describing the same trip over the Alps, could express himself in contradic-
tory terms:

> I am just now arriv'd at Geneva by a very troublesome Journey over the
> Alpes where I have bin for some days together shivering among the Eternal
> Snows. My head is still Giddy with mountains and precipices and you cant
> Imagine how much I am pleas'd with the sight of a Plain.

> I came directly from *Turin* to *Geneva,* and had a very easie journey over
> mount *Cennis,* though about the beginning of *December,* the snows having
> not yet fallen. On the tip of this high mountain is a large Plain, and in the
> midst of the plain a beautiful Lake.... There is nothing in the natural
> face of *Italy* that is more delightful to a traveller, than the several Lakes
> which are dispersed up and down among the many breaks and hollows of
> the *Alpes* and *Appennines.*

Addison's letter to Edward Montagu, from which the first quotation
is taken, indicates that his feelings for the Alps were dominated by
his discomfort in the cold and his lightheadedness in the heights; *Remarks on Italy,* from which the second is taken, reveals a delighted
—if rather impersonal—appreciation of the identical landscape.[23]
We probably will never be able to determine Addison's real feelings,
which very likely differ little from those of most travelers: a mixture
of distaste for the inconveniences caused by the Alps and pleasure
for the sense of sublimity they inspire.

The criticisms leveled at Addison's narrative and descriptive passages thus do not comprehend accurately the artistry of his book.
Literary conventions gradually changed, and as they did, evaluations of Addison's book progressively became more and more severe.
While the *Spectator* praised *Remarks on Italy* in 1712 as being "one
of the most entertaining Pieces this Age has produc'd," Dr. Johnson

ultimately found in 1773 that it was "a tedious book" to read. To a large extent, as we shall see, literary conventions and rhetorical techniques developed during the century in such a manner that later readers did not quite understand the generic conventions Addison was trying to follow. Indeed, the anonymous editor of the 1830 *Miscellaneous Works of Joseph Addison* seems to be the last person, at least in print, who clearly recognized the genre in which Addison was writing his *Remarks.* In explaining early nineteenth-century attitudes toward *Remarks on Italy,* this editor asserts that Addison's account is "little in accordance with the style of modern travel writings, but to turn from their sickly sentiment, deceptive morality, and fictitious adventures, to the chaste and unaffected narrative of Addison is, as it has been beautifully remarked, like 'being recalled to a sense of something like that original purity from which man has been long estranged.'" Although overwrought, this evaluation of the changes that had occurred in travel literature between 1705 and 1830 helps explain why subsequent generations have misinterpreted the significance of a number of statements both in *Remarks on Italy* and, more important, in eighteenth-century travel literature in general. Addison's "journal of poetical travels," as Tickell calls it,[24] shows how fundamental problems arise when readers do not comprehend the conventional aims of travel literature and when literary historians are ignorant of the tradition in which travelers write.

### *Fiction and Nonfiction: The Case of* Humphry Clinker *and* Travels through France and Italy

In order to arrive at the eighteenth century's definition of nonfiction travel literature, one must first of all distinguish factual accounts from the fictional works that time and again delighted readers. Percy Adams's *Travelers and Travel Liars* identifies three kinds of travel books on the basis of their contents. William Dampier's *New Voyage round the World* (1697), what Adams classifies as a "true travel account," accurately reports Dampier's genuine experiences and observations. In contrast, *Gulliver's Travels* is an "imaginary, or extraordinary, voyage," the kind of literary work treated at length

in Philip Babcock Gove's *Imaginary Voyage in Prose Fiction*. Any
reader with the slightest sophistication, claims Adams, soon recognizes the fictional nature of Swift's satire since six-inch Lilliputians,
floating islands, and talking horses defy belief. A third and less
easily defined kind of travel literature is what Adams calls the
"travel lie." William Symson's *New Voyage to the East-Indies*
(1715), for example, is a fiction, since Symson was not a real person
and since much of the narrative consists of passages stolen from
other writers. Nevertheless, Symson's work appears to be a "true
travel account"; no one but an expert in travel literature would
recognize its fictional contents. This presentation of fiction under
the guise of truth justifies its classification as a travel lie.[25]

Such distinctions based purely on subject matter depend ultimately upon the reader's ability to discern truth from cunning fiction. Although Adams ferrets out the most important travel lies of
the century, he is forced to rely upon artistic intuitions when classifying a work like Arthur Young's *Travels in France* (1792) as a "true
account." Young, for instance, says that on 22 June 1789 he dined
"with the Duc de Liancourt, in the palace" together with "a large
party of nobility and deputies of the Commons" including the duc
d'Orléans, the bishop of Rodez, Abbé Sieyès, and M. Rabaut-St-
Étienne. Because we have no way of demonstrating that Young
actually broke bread with all these men, our classification of his
book on the basis of its contents must necessarily remain conjectural.
As Samuel Paterson points out in his lively parody of eighteenth-
century travel accounts, a gentleman may introduce into his book
"persons and characters as familiars, whom, perhaps, he never saw
— and nobody can contradict him."[26] Likewise, *Remarks on Italy*
may well be a travel lie since, for one thing, Addison incorrectly
states he was in Venice on Holy Thursday. We recognize this "lie"—
if in fact it is a lie and not a careless mistake—because of the inconsistencies in his dates.[27] But if Addison stretches the truth here, he
might just as easily have done so in less detectable places. We cannot, for instance, determine with any certainty that he actually
visited the Grotto del Cani near Naples (p. 112). An acquaintance
might have told him about the famous experiments in the cave, or
he might well have read about them in any number of contemporary

accounts like Misson's *Nouveau voyage d'Italie* (1691), Bourdin's *Voyage d'Italie* (1699), and Montfaucon's *Diarium italicum* (1702). "Because there have been lying travellers," proclaimed the *Critical Review* in 1770, "the veracity of almost every traveller is suspected." The reader, as a consequence, must rely on his "judgment to discriminate betwixt appearance and reality" when deciding whether to trust a travel account.[28]

Thus it is difficult if not impossible to make fine distinctions on the basis of content alone, since all such categories presuppose omniscience. Classifications based on form, however, usually avoid these practically insurmountable problems. No sophisticated reader, after all, can fail to see that Dampier's *New Voyage* and Smollett's *Travels through France and Italy* (1766) are basically nonfiction travel accounts. While these works may partly be fictional, and while they may report some lies, they nevertheless conform to the formal pattern of eighteenth-century nonfiction travel literature. Here we must follow Dr. Johnson's commonsense advice: since Father Jeronymo Lobo amused readers "with no Romantick Absurdities or Incredible Fictions" in his *Voyage to Abyssinia* (French 1728; English 1735), everything he says, "whether true or not, is at least probable." For this reason, Lobo has a right to demand, according to Johnson, "that they should believe him, who cannot contradict him."[29]

But while Johnson's is a generally sound approach to classifying eighteenth-century travel literature, it raises problems when it is applied to a work like Smollett's *Expedition of Humphry Clinker,* which borrows the form we associate with travel accounts and a kind of obvious fictionality we associate with novels. Because of this hybrid nature, *Humphry Clinker* has caused a degree of uneasiness specifically among critics who have tried to classify it as a novel. While its narrative has always pleased readers, it nevertheless lacks the type of unity we have come to expect in successful novels. *Humphry Clinker* fails, in fact, to follow Smollett's own definition of the novel. Although it portrays "a large diffused picture, comprehending the characters of life, disposed in different groupes, and exhibited in various attitudes, for the purposes of an uniform plan," it also contains lengthy descriptions of geographical settings — forming roughly one-half of the work—which contribute little to unwinding what Smollett calls the narrative "clue of the labyrinth."[30]

The search for a novelistic form has unfortunately led either to complaints that *Humphry Clinker* is a seriously flawed work or to discoveries of obscure signs that supposedly open up its artistic maze. Sheldon Sacks, for example, dismisses Smollett's work as an unsuccessful action "with so many digressions of one kind and another that its total effect" is "somewhat vitiated." B. L. Reid, in contrast, sees *Humphry Clinker* as a unified novel of character development in which characters move "from negative to positive, from passive to active: sickness to health, constipation to purgation . . . ignorance to knowledge." Finally, M. A. Goldberg attempts to save its artistic reputation by interpreting *Humphry Clinker* as a kind of apologue in which the virtues of rural life are held up as a moral and social lesson for the reader.[31]

While Smollett certainly develops plot, character, and thought in *Humphry Clinker*, none of these is clearly the central, controlling concern of the literary work. In fact, to judge from its opening pages, Smollett thought of *Humphry Clinker* more in terms of a travel book than a novel. He begins it with the business communications between the Reverend Jonathan Dustwich, supposed possessor of the letters that comprise *Humphry Clinker*, and Henry Davis, the London bookseller who is supposedly negotiating to print them. Davis, unwilling to pay Dustwich more than half the profits of the impression, explains his fear of losing money in such an undertaking, especially when he considers how "the taste of the town is so changeable." He further laments that "there have been so many letters upon travels lately published—What between Smollett's, Sharp's, Derrick's, Thicknesse's, Baltimore's and Baretti's, together with Shandy's Sentimental Travels, the public seems to be cloyed with that kind of entertainment." In these ironic introductory remarks, Smollett points to the close relationship *Humphry Clinker* and Sterne's *Sentimental Journey* share with such nonfiction travel accounts as his own *Travels through France and Italy*, Samuel Sharp's *Letters from Italy* (1766), Samuel Derrick's *Letters Written from Leverpoole* (1767), Philip Thicknesse's *Observations on the Customs and Manners of the French Nation* (1766) and *Useful Hints to Those Who Make the Tour of France* (1768), Lord Baltimore's *Tour to the East* (1767), and Giuseppe Baretti's *Journey from London to Genoa* (1770).

In identifying *Humphry Clinker* with these nonfiction travel accounts, Smollett clearly did not wish to disguise his fiction as a collection of authentic letters. His title page, after all, reads: *The Expedition of Humphry Clinker. By the Author of Roderick Random.* But while its characters and events are patently fictional, Smollett's relatives immediately saw *Humphry Clinker* as "only a history, fictitiously coloured," of the trip he took to his native Scotland in the spring of 1766.[32] Indeed, almost every commentator on the work has pointed out similarities between Smollett and Matthew Bramble, his fictional counterpart: they are the same age and suffer from the same ill health; they express similar attitudes concerning numerous subjects; they have many of the same friends; and, above all, their personalities are almost identical.[33] Furthermore, real people — hidden under no disguise whatsoever — appear in the fictional *Humphry Clinker:* we see the duke of Newcastle, Samuel Derrick, Charles Townshend, Dr. John Moore, and James Quin, to name only a few. Furthermore, since the dates and places mentioned in the letters that comprise *Humphry Clinker* generally correspond with the limited information we have about Smollett's Scottish trip, we may conjecture that he probably based *Humphry Clinker* either on a diary or journal kept during his excursion.

We encounter a similar mixture of fact and fiction in Smollett's supposedly nonfictional *Travels through France and Italy.* The letters comprising it purport to be Smollett's private correspondence written from Europe to friends back in England. His first letter begins: "You laid your commands upon me at parting, to communicate from time to time the observations I should make in the course of my travels." But this statement is a palpable fiction. Six months before his *Travels* appeared, he wrote Dr. Moore saying, "The observations I made in the course of my Travels thro' France and Italy *I have thrown into a Series of Letters.*"[34] In pretending to publish his "genuine" travel letters written from the Continent, Smollett simply follows an accepted literary ploy found in many travel accounts. And while his descriptions of France and Italy seem factual enough, occasional inconsistencies in his letters prove that he could not have written them from the Continent as he wishes his readers to suppose.

Attempts to discern fact from fiction in both works, then, reduce critics to petty detectives. But any sophisticated eighteenth-century reader would have intuited the fundamental generic distinction between these works and would therefore have approached them in a different fashion. *Travels through France and Italy* is a nonfiction travel book because in content and form it imitates the authentic travel accounts published during the mid-eighteenth century. Smollett's *Travels* primarily contains a description of those parts of France and Italy which he seems to have visited. Furthermore, these descriptions and the philosophical reflections they occasion are organized in an autobiographical manner: the author describes and comments upon "Character, Customs, Religion, Government, Police, Commerce, Arts, and Antiquities"[35] in the order in which he appears to have observed them during the course of his journey. Smollett's *Travels*—like most eighteenth-century nonfiction travels—contains some anecdotes and personal experiences, but these are clearly subservient in importance to the descriptions of France and Italy. Likewise, an eighteenth-century reader would probably have recognized that *Humphry Clinker* is a fictional travel book because, while conforming to most of the characteristics of the authentic travel account, it deviates in three important respects: it contains a plot, it is too "egotistical" in relating personal opinions and insignificant experiences, and it contains letters written by more than one person which reveal varying points of view concerning the people and places visited.


Utile Dulce: *Travel Books as Literature*


Unlike subsequent centuries, the eighteenth century quite consistently saw the factual travel account as being of distinct literary merit. A writer like Defoe could scarcely agree with the modern sentiment that "no one expects literature in a book of travel."[36] Indeed, by prefacing his *Tour thro' the Whole Island of Great Britain* (1724-

1727) with a statement that his work should provide both pleasure and instruction, Defoe aims at satisfying Horace's famous literary dictum, *Omne tulit punctum qui miscuit utile dulci / Lectorem delectando pariterque monendo*, which often went hand in hand with Horace's *prodesse et delectare* in order to define desired literary effects. Impassioned pleas for pleasurable instruction appeared from the pens of such thinkers as Plato, Sidney, and Dryden, this ideal ultimately becoming one of the acknowledged cornerstones of neoclassical criticism. The main problem—or perhaps virtue—of this artistic formula was the vagueness of its meaning, which changed in the hands of different interpreters. For some, *pleasure* might mean no more than the emotion derived from learning things, and for others, *instruction* might be the teaching of such different subjects as "the good, the useful, the true, and the beautiful."[37] But in any event, the application of *utile dulce* to travel literature during the eighteenth century elevated the genre to the rank of poesy, an artistic category that traditionally had included, among others, such genres as epic, tragedy, and comedy.

To be certain, a few travel accounts during the first half of the century claim, like Daniel Beeckman's *Voyage to and from the Island of Borneo* (1718), "to have a greater regard to Utility than Pleasure," but they usually do so in an attempt to avoid the appearance of being "the Bundle of Lies" so frequently published by earlier travelers. If an eighteenth-century travel account honestly aims solely at instructing its readers, it is an infrequent one like Pascoe Thomas's *True and Impartial Journal of a Voyage to the South-Seas* (1745), professedly written only for voyagers who plan to follow the same path. With a specialized audience in mind, Thomas refuses to narrate "Sufferings and Hardships on the Voyage," restricting his account to only such practical information as will assist subsequent circumnavigations. This limited goal leads Thomas to sacrifice both pleasure and all kinds of instruction save the merely practical, making the objectives of his account little more than those of a Baedeker. But the travel account directed at the general reader, the one in search of something more than assistance in preparing for his own travels, always aimed at blending pleasure with instruction in order to achieve an artistically pleasing literary experience. For this reason, travels formed an important portion of the ideal eighteenth-century library.[38]

To judge from its popularity throughout the entire century, Defoe's *Tour thro' the Whole Island of Great Britain* achieved precisely the literary aims dictated by Horace, but in order to do so Defoe introduced some fiction into his travel account.[39] In fact, the itinerary Defoe reports having followed serves as a central fiction by which he draws together both personal observations gleaned from various trips through Great Britain as well as facts often taken without acknowledgment from other books. Consequently, Defoe's descriptions *seem* essentially truthful, but the narrative that connects them is largely fictional. Yet instead of casting doubt on the instructional value of the whole work, the fictionality of the narrative serves to make the travel book more pleasing. The narrative unites and orders his descriptions; through it Defoe presents, in a pleasing manner, descriptions that should be instructionally profitable to his readers.

Henry Fielding also quotes Horace's dictum at the beginning of his travel account, but Fielding paraphrases it in order to explain the difficulties inherent in virtually all travel literature: "There would not, perhaps, be a more pleasant, or profitable study, among those which have their principle end in amusement, than that of travels or voyages, if they be writ, as they might be, and ought to be, with a joint view to the entertainment and information of mankind." Few travelers know what kind of information to collect, he stresses, and fewer still can express such information in a pleasing manner. For this reason, many travel accounts lack real literary merit: instead of providing readers with pleasant instruction, they simply furnish dull trivialities.[40]

In proposing "to convey instruction in the vehicle of entertainment,"[41] Fielding defines the major criterion used by reviewers of travel books during the eighteenth century. Voyages and travels that both please and instruct always receive praise, sometimes in rather extravagant terms. "A book of travels, in which materials are in general important, and well managed," according to the *Critical Review,* is one of the most entertaining and instructive of literary productions. There is a happy mixture in it of the *utile* and the *dulce;* it amuses and captivates our fancy, without the fiction of romance; it gives us a large proportion of moral and political information, without the tediousness and perplexity of system. It promotes and facilitates the intercourse of countries remote from each other; it dispels from our minds unreasonable and gloomy antipathies against those manners, customs, forms of government, and religion, to which we have not been bred: it makes man mild, and sociable to man; it makes us consider ourselves and all mankind as brethren, the workmanship of one Supreme benign Creator; a truth as obvious to reflection as neglected in conduct.

Assuming the role of physician, the *Critical Review* went so far as to prescribe travel literature as a particularly healthful regimen for readers: "There cannot be an easier or more wholesome diet for boundless curiosity, than the mental entertainment" in travels, "where pleasure and instruction go hand in hand." Less flamboyant commentary frequently judged travel accounts superior to fiction because of the special way they unite pleasure and instruction. Thus one reviewer in 1756 thought that travels would "for the most part, afford us a much more rational entertainment than the fashionable study of idle novels and romances, which are perpetually pouring in upon us." And eight years later, in praising *The Beauties of Nature and Art Displayed: In a Tour through the World* (1763-1764) for uniting utility with pleasure, another reviewer pointed out that "nothing in the regions of romance or fiction" can provide "greater pleasure than what a real description of Nature herself can offer." Fictions are inferior to travels, he proclaimed, because in reading them "the mind is generally crouded with images that, even allowing them to be innocent, we ought to banish, as they take up that room which more useful subjects require." By studying travel books, however, "we fill up many disagreeable intervals of time with a study which will always entertain and improve the understanding."[42] In fact, travels are so pleasurable that they can even seduce readers into useful activities: the entertainment arising from them "has often fixed the minds of persons, who had before no relish for learning, and brought them by degrees to enter upon closer studies, in order to gratify that curiosity which this kind of reading naturally excites." For these reasons, reviewers and editors—together with clergymen—frequently recommended travel accounts, especially for the youthful or inexperienced or female reader.[43]

While eighteenth-century reviewers consistently praise travel books that pleasantly instruct and condemn those that fail in this objective,[44] they encounter serious problems when evaluating accounts that instruct without pleasing or please without instructing. Though praising the usefulness of Constantine John Phipps's *Voyage towards the North Pole* (1774), the *Critical Review* finally must confess that it contains little entertainment since Phipps "confined his narrative to the great and useful objects of science, for the ascertainment of which the voyage had been projected. Intent on the improvement of navigation, geography, and natural history, it was his purpose to give a faithful detail of such facts and observations as materially conduced to answer the end of the undertaking." With a particularized audience in mind, Phipps selected only details that would instruct readers primarily interested in scientific and navigational information. In sharp contrast, an anonymous account of the same voyage had appeared shortly before Phipps's did, but this *Journal of a Voyage* (1773), because it was directed at a general audience, aims "rather at gratifying the curiosity with novelty and anecdote, than disseminating useful information." Considering this limited objective, the reviewer admits that this work "is properly enough conducted," and those people "such as read chiefly for amusement, or the gratification which uncommon occurrences afford, will not be displeased with this narrative."[45] In effect, the *Critical Review* praises both voyages, yet the one primarily instructs while the other primarily entertains. Toward the end of the century, reviewers increasingly do not prima facie dismiss works that fail to satisfy both demands together. Thus the *Monthly Review* recommends *Relation d'un voyage de Paris* (1770), in spite of its uninstructive nature, to those "who read merely for amusement," while the *Analytical Review* praises Joseph Townsend's *Journey through Spain* (1791), even though it lacks amusement, for those with inquisitive minds.[46] But still, a book like Baron Inigo Born's *Travels through the Bannat of Temeswar* (German 1774; English 1777) always receives highest praise because of its adherence to the "excellent Horatian rule" even in treating the instructive and abstruse subject of mineralogy.[47]

Only with the advent of the "picturesque traveller" in the 1780s and 1790s did these rigid criteria significantly change. In the accounts of William Gilpin and his followers, we find for the first time nonfiction descriptions directed simply for the entertainment of readers. Earlier travelers, to be certain, had described natural settings, but always with the objective of joining instruction with pleasure, and never with the picturesque aim of arousing in their readers an emotional response to the beauties of a particular geographical location. In this respect, travelers and topographical poets of the earlier part of the century are strikingly similar. Defoe may describe Windsor Forest, but only to give factual information about it. Pope may describe the same place in decidedly more evocative terms, but his main objective is not the description per se, but the use of this description to explain England's peace and hopeful prosperity after the Treaty of Utrecht. By the end of the century, however, Gilpin and others had begun to examine "the face of the country *by the rules of picturesque beauty*" in order to open up sublime pleasures for their readers. For example, John Hassell claims that from "a Tour of this kind, in which the beauties of Nature are the object of our search, we experience a pleasure that few amusements can furnish." Even when Hassell includes factual information about antiquities, commerce, and the like, he justifies it as entertainment: it tends to relieve the monotony of his main subject. These travel accounts, of course, earned their share of criticism from the more traditional-minded readers. For example, the English translator of Moritz's *Travels* (German 1783; English 1795) took exception with the false taste of travelers who, with "degrading condescension," aim simply at entertaining readers with "the fairey scenes of picturesque beauty."[48] But the great popularity of these works more than argued against the effectiveness of such criticism.

This shift, initially slow in coming, signaled a change in the course of subsequent books written by and for travelers. In the opening decades of the nineteenth century, two kinds of accounts achieved prominence: the purely entertaining travel book and the

instructive travel guide. To be certain, exclusively entertaining
travel books had existed since the 1780s, and informative travel
guides date back further than the seventeenth century,[49] but now,
pleasure clearly becomes divorced from instruction in travel literature. Marianna Starke's frequently revised travel books and guides
clearly reflect the peculiarly uneasy state of travel literature at the
beginning of the nineteenth century. When her *Letters from Italy*
appeared in 1800, Dr. Burney promptly complained that its opening letter, with its effusively picturesque description of the Alps, was
pleasant but not instructive. Other reviewers thought the rest of the
book instructive, but scarcely pleasing. Information about such
practical matters as the "best shops for perfumery," complained one
such critic, would better have been "printed in a convenient size for
a post-chaise pocket under the title of the Traveller's Guide — not
swollen into octavo volumes, and called Letters from Italy."[50] Heed-
ing such criticism, Mrs. Starke gradually dropped all literary pre-
texts in her subsequent works. As the revised title page states, she
carefully "adapted" her *Travels in Europe* (1828) for "the Use of
Travellers," giving few details about herself while conveying veritable masses of useful information about Europe. Indeed, by the time
the eighth edition of her *Travels in Europe* appeared in 1832, Mrs.
Starke had so thoroughly eliminated the autobiographical organization of her book that it had become a travel guide, indistinguishable
from a Murray or a Baedeker.

The nineteenth century nevertheless saw a modicum of "literary"
travel accounts, like Kinglake's *Eöthen* and Beckford's *Italy; with
Sketches of Spain and Portugal* (1834), but most of these contain
decidedly fewer facts than the standard eighteenth-century travel
book. Indeed, Beckford's *Italy* clearly reflects the transition between
the eighteenth and nineteenth centuries in terms of pleasure and
instruction. Originally published as *Dreams, Waking Thoughts and
Incidents* in 1783, most of Beckford's 500 copies were immediately
burned, apparently at the insistence of his parents. Biographers
have offered hypotheses to explain this conflagration: that his irate
parents feared the book would compromise Beckford's parliamen-
tary career, that its criticisms of the Dutch would offend prominent
political figures, and the like.[51] In any event, Beckford's *Dreams*

scarcely conforms with accepted eighteenth-century literary conventions: it relates too much about Beckford, too little about the places he visited. Even when he again published the book in 1834, he revised it extensively to tone down its autobiographical effusions. As an entertaining account of its author—rather than the countries he visited—*Dreams* initially appeared some fifty years before its time.

### The Eighteenth-Century Travel Book
### as a Literary Genre

The sense of literary kind or species was central to the criticism of the eighteenth century. Though Dr. Johnson could complain that "scarcely any species of writing" exists "of which we can tell what is its essence and what are its constituents," he nevertheless on the heels of such a statement could take a commonsense generic approach when attacking the contemporary abuses of a particular literary kind. In part, the century's fascination with genre derived from a sense that decorum to some extent governed each literary form: authors could accomplish certain objectives in one kind of literature which they scarcely could achieve in another. Generic conventions, however, necessarily shifted as new authors cast about for novelty within the traditional forms. Each new writer of genius, explains Johnson, "produces some innovation which, when invented and approved, subverts the rules which the practice of foregoing authors established."[52] Thus the reader's understanding of each literary work depends upon his intuitions not only of the unique intentions of its author but also of the traditional objectives of the literary form in which the author wrote. Though invariable literary strictures clearly do not exist, some sense of the rules established by previous authors is essential to governing the attempts of each author and the understandings of each reader.

In distinguishing between fictional and nonfictional travel books and in describing the "literary" nature of travel accounts, we have assumed these works are easily distinguishable from such literary genres as the novel, the biography, and the descriptive geography. The travel book's autobiographically determined narrative, however, suggests that it is merely a specialized form of biography describing the events in an author's life during a trip. Fielding's *Journal of a Voyage to Lisbon* (1755) is certainly autobiographical to the extent that it "contains an account of the adventures and distresses of the author and his family, in a journey."[53] Yet travel books also bear a striking resemblance to descriptive geographies in their treatment of such subjects as the physical appearance, customs, commerce, history, and laws of specific areas. To this extent, the title page of Defoe's *Tour* might well catalog the contents of any number of geographical studies:

I.   A Description of the Principal Cities and Towns, their Situation, Magnitude, Government, and Commerce.
II.   The Customs, Manners, Speech, as also the Exercises, Divisions, and Employment of the People.
III.   The Produce and Improvement of the Lands, the Trade, and Manufactures.
IV.   The Sea Parts and Fortifications, the Course of Rivers, and the Inland Navigation.
V.   The Publick Edifices, Seats, and Palaces of the Nobility and Gentry. *With Useful* Observations *upon the Whole.*[54]

Despite these similarities to other conventional genres, the travel book seemed an easily distinguishable literary form to eighteenth-century readers. "Voyages and Travels," said Abraham Rees in 1771, "are a species of instruction, which is generally acceptable and amusing; they gratify that love of novelty and variety, which is natural to the human mind." Three years later, John Langhorne referred to them as "a particular species of entertainment."[55] And toward the end of the century, Arthur Young introduced his *Travels in France* by distinguishing between two kinds of travels. After undertaking a journey, an author may publish either a register of the journey itself or a description of the results of the trip: "In the former case, it is a diary, under which head are to be classed all those books of travels written in the form of letters. The latter usually falls into the shape of essays on distinct subjects." After explaining that "almost every book of modern travels" is a "register," Young examines the relative merits of the two methods of writing:

The journal form hath the advantage of carrying with it a greater degree of credibility; and, of course, more weight. A traveller who thus registers his observations is detected the moment he writes of things he has not seen. He is precluded from giving studied or elaborate remarks upon insufficient foundations. If he sees little, he must register little; if he has few good opportunities of being well-informed, the reader is enabled to observe it, and will be induced to give no more credit to his relations than the sources of them appear to deserve. If he passes so rapidly through a country as necessarily to be no judge of what he sees, the reader knows it; if he dwells long in places of little or no moment with private views or for private business, the circumstance is seen; and thus the reader has the satisfaction of being as safe from imposition either designed or involuntary, as the nature of the case will admit; all which advantages are wanted in the other method.

This journal form, nevertheless, has some "weighty inconveniencies." Most especially, it leads to a prolixity, causing the author to repeat himself frequently, and it forces him to convey important information "by scraps as received," not in an ordered and connected argument. In the essay form, on the contrary,

there is this obvious and great advantage, that the subjects thus treated are in as complete a state of combination and illustration as the abilities of the author can make them; the matter comes with full force and effect. Another admirable circumstance is brevity; for by the rejection of all useless details, the reader has nothing before him but what tends to the full explanation of the subject. Of the disadvantages, I need not speak; they are sufficiently noted by showing the benefits of the diary form; but proportionably to the benefits of the one, will clearly be the disadvantages of the other.

Young uses this discussion to explain how he could retain the benefits of both plans by dividing his *Travels* into two sections, the first assuming the form of a "Journal" and the second the form of "General Observations." The Journal, arranged autobiographically, contains particular observations and reflections on France, with "trifling" incidents and a "variety of little circumstances" he threw "upon paper for the amusement" of family and friends. The section entitled General Observations, arranged in chapters according to various topics, describes "Soil," "Face of the Country," "Population," "Capital Employed in Husbandry," and the like. Young confesses that he had originally intended to expurgate trivial and personal information from the first section of *Travels in France,* but was advised against it by a friend who felt such details "would best please the mass of common readers." The autobiographical section of *Travels in France,* as a consequence, aims at pleasing the general reader, the one with no particular interest in agricultural matters. The scientific section containing general observations, however, aims at instructing readers with specialized interests. With this mixture, Young successfully overcame the problems he encountered in *A Tour in Ireland* (1780), which failed to interest the general public even though it was, as a friend opined, *"one of the best accounts"* of any country.[56]

Dividing *Travels in France* in this manner, Young did not invent, despite what he implies, a new way of writing travel books. James Boswell had composed his *Account of Corsica* in 1768 using the same format but reversing the order so that his autobiographical section came last. In an explanation that reads suspiciously like a first draft of Young's Preface, Boswell declares twenty-four years before Young that his first intention was "to give only a view of the present state of Corsica, together with the Memoirs of its illustrious General"; but prompted "by the advice of some learned friends," he altered his plan, adding an autobiographical section entitled "The Journal of a Tour to That Island."[57] Boswell's ardently desired literary fame, of which he speaks so candidly in his Preface, came precisely from this added portion of *An Account of Corsica.* The first part of his book, according to Dr. Johnson, is like other natural histories, but his "Journal is in a very high degree curious and delightful." Johnson further explains to Boswell:

There is between the history and the journal that difference which there will always be found between notions borrowed from without, and notions generated within. Your history was copied from books; your journal rose out of your own experience and observation. You express images which operated strongly upon yourself, and you have impressed them with great force upon your readers. I know not whether I could name any narrative by which curiosity is better excited, or better gratified.[58]

Johnson makes the same distinctions here that Boswell and Young employ. The first part of *An Account of Corsica* may be important and instructive with its discussions of "the Situation, Extent, Air, Soil, and Productions, of Corsica,"[59] but it does not provide the entertaining instructions of the second part. Dr. Johnson had seen this kind of arrangement in Father Lobo's *Voyage historique d'Abissinie* (1728), which he translated into English in 1735, and he might well have known of similar combinations of narrative and nonnarrative sections in such travel accounts as Baron Lahontan's *New Voyages to North-America* (French 1703; English 1703), John Lawson's *New Voyage to Carolina* (1709), and Henry Ellis's *Voyage to Hudson's-Bay* (1748). A work like John Green's *Journey from Aleppo to Damascus* (1736) indeed devotes only a brief chapter to narrating travel experiences, the preponderance of the book being a collection of miscellaneous information about Syria.

While Young considers as travel books both the "register of the journey" and its "result," most of his contemporaries would have disagreed that the "result," when appearing alone, should be classified as such. In *Adventurer* 4, for instance, John Hawkesworth distinguishes eight kinds of narrative compositions: histories, voyages and travels, biographies, epic poems, novels, tales of Genii and Fairies, dramatic poems, and brief stories published in periodicals. Hawkesworth then defines the qualities essential to these narrative genres:

It is always necessary, that facts should appear to be produced in a regular and connected series, that they should follow in a quick succession, and yet that they should be delivered with discriminating circumstances. If they have not a necessary and apparent connection, the ideas which they excite obliterate each other, and the mind is tantalized with an imperfect glimpse of innumerable objects that just appear and vanish; if they are too minutely related, they become tiresome; and if divested of all their circumstances, insipid; for who that reads, in a table of chronology or an index, that a city was swallowed up by an earthquake, or a kingdom depopulated by a pestilence, finds either his attention engaged, or his curiosity gratified?

According to Hawkesworth, John Symonds's essay "Upon the Soil of Italy"—which Young classifies as the "result" of travel—would not

be a travel account since, lacking a narrative, it simply describes in
random order the various kinds of earths found in Italy. The facts
concerning this subject are not, as Hawkesworth would say, "delivered with discriminating circumstances," and hence this work
scarcely provides "general entertainment."[60]

Essential, then, to travel literature is this narrative ordering of
details. Depending upon the date of publication and the status of
the author, the acceptable amount of narrative information might
indeed vary from one account to another, but the presence of at
least a minimal narrative was one of the necessary attributes of the
genre. Thus the *Critical Review* complains that Francis Carter's
*Journey from Gibraltar to Malaga* (1777), "though intitled a Journey, is not written in the manner of an historical narrative." "Divided into various heads which contain the accounts of ancient and
modern towns, unconnected with each other," it lacks the organizing principle necessary in travel books. Discussing Jacques Brissot de
Warville's *New Travels in the United States of America* (French
1791; English 1792-1794), another reviewer indicates that its second
volume is not actually a travel account, but rather a series of reflections the author has massed together. Similarly, the *Critical Review*
attacks *Voyage de deux Français* (1796) for not being, "properly
speaking, a book of travels, but what is now called a statistical
account of each country, geographical, political, commercial and
literary." Though this *Voyage* begins like a narrative with "En
sortant de Strasbourg, nous avons passé le Rhin,"[61] all autobiographical references to *nous* or *je* immediately disappear.

The eighteenth century considered as "literary" only those books
written by travelers who employed a narrative organization. For this
reason, travel guides clearly do not form a subclass of travel literature. A work like Thomas Nugent's *Grand Tour* (1749), despite the
term *tour* in its title, is simply a compilation of information that
would be of assistance to travelers undertaking specific trips. The
same can be said of such popular works as Daniel Paterson's *Travelling Dictionary* (1772), John Millard's *Gentleman's Guide in His
Tour through France* (1768), and itineraries like those of Antonius
and Leland. The initial entries in the table of contents for Millard's
book give a clear picture of the purely utilitarian nature of these
guides:

*General Remarks necessary to be read by a Gentleman who designs to travel; with an accurate Account of the* French *Coins,*
*From* London *to* Calais,
*From* Calais *to* Paris, *through* Abbeville,
*From* Calais *to* Paris, *by the Way of* Lisle, *through* Dunkirk *and* Ypres,
*Another Road to* Lisle, *through St.* Omer's, *which is the nearest,*
*From* London *to* Paris, *by Way of* Brighthelmstone *in* Sussex, *to* Dieppe, *through* Rouen *in* Normandy.[62]

Aimed only at a specialized audience looking for practical help while traveling, these works include much that is useful, but nothing that is entertaining. For this reason, the *Analytical Review* refused to classify as literature travel guides and notes jotted down solely to refresh the memory of travelers.[63]

Titles, as we see, can be misleading. While some works falsely appear to be travel books, others have titles that obscure their true genre. Addison, for example, probably modeled the title of his account after William Bromley's *Remarks in the Grande Tour of France & Italy* (1692), a genuine travel book. Yet in spite of its similar title, Andrew Lumisden's *Remarks on the Antiquities of Rome* (1797) bears little formal similarity to the *Remarks* of Bromley, Addison, or Breval. Not ordered on an autobiographical principle, Lumisden's *Remarks* describes Rome using the following format: (1) the gates of Rome, (2) the hills of Rome, (3) the "circumjacent plains," (4) the Tiber and its bridges, and (5) the Transtiberim suburb. The title of Dr. John Moore's *View of Society and Manners in France* (1779), however, first confused readers into expecting "a formal dissertation, of a political and moral kind, not the incidental remarks of a traveller, made in performing the grand tour, and published in a series of familiar letters."[64] But Moore's *View* is a "narrative," not a "dissertation" like Gilbert Stuart's *View of Society in Europe,* which appeared the year before Moore's work. Likewise, while William Gilpin's numerous "observations" are genuine travel books (e.g., *Observations on the River Wye* [1782], *Observations on the Western Parts of England* [1798]), the "picturesque views" of his imitator Samuel Ireland lack this essential narrative structure (e.g., *Picturesque Views on the River Thames* [1791], *Picturesque Views on the River Wye* [1797]). Gilpin organizes his works according to his own travels, Ireland according to the flow of rivers from their sources to their mouths or vice versa. Frequently, however, one of several virtually synonymous terms — like *travels, journey, voyage,* or *tour* — appears somewhere in a title. While *travels* and *journey* carry no specific connotations, *voyage* usually describes a sea trip, and *tour* almost always narrates a trip during which the traveler completes a circuit, returning to the point from which he originally departed. Even so, travelers used these terms so often and in so many ways that they became interchangeable and hopelessly confused. Thus Richard Lassels spends no time on a ship in his *Voyage of Italy* (1670), and John Ferrar never again sees the shores of Ireland in his *Tour from Dublin to London* (1796).

Eighteenth-century authors used two basic techniques in organizing their travel accounts as narratives. Fielding's *Journal of a Voyage to Lisbon* and Addison's *Remarks on Italy,* on the one hand, appear in the form of journals. This format is more obvious in Fielding's *Voyage,* which preserves the semblance of a journal so closely that it lists all descriptions under the headings of dates. Addison, however, pays practically no attention to dates, dividing his *Remarks* into chapters, each dealing with a part of Italy or Switzerland which he visited. But since he describes these countries in the order in which he seems to have made his trip, *Remarks on Italy* basically resembles a journal.[65] On the other hand, travel books like Smollett's *Travels through France and Italy* and Brydone's *Tour through Sicily and Malta* assume an epistolary form. Some, like Smollett's, consist of letters addressed to a number of different correspondents; others, like Brydone's, contain letters addressed to a single person. At times this distinction between journals and letters becomes cloudy. William Dalrymple, for example, published his *Travels through Spain and Portugal* (1777) in the form of letters, confessing nevertheless that they were simply transcriptions from his journal.[66] Such differences, however, are scarcely fundamental in defining travel books as a literary genre. Journals and letters both narrate the experiences of their authors; for this reason, Arthur Young classified epistolary travel accounts under the heading of "diaries," and the *Monthly Review* opined that "the form of a journal" is "the natural form for travels.[67]

Eighteenth-century reviewers, nevertheless, frequently condemn travel books that seem too autobiographical. Thus Oliver Goldsmith found fault with one such work because its author lapsed into recounting his actions rather than describing previously unknown cities, towns, ruins, mountains, and rivers. After all, asks Goldsmith, "What information can be received from hearing" that a traveler "went up such an hill, only in order to come down again?"[68] The *Critical Review* likewise condemns Philip Thicknesse's *Observations on the Customs and Manners of the French Nation* for containing "hackneyed encomiums upon himself," and his *Useful Hints to Those Who Make the Tour of France* for being full of "conceited egotisms." In the same vein, Gilbert Stuart attacks books written by adventurers; while most travel accounts convey instruction and entertainment, those written by such men are "almost always personal" and thus "have little that can amuse or interest" the reader. By the time Mrs. Piozzi published her *Observations and Reflections* in 1789, the general configurations of eighteenth-century travel literature were beginning to change, allowing for the introduction of increasing amounts of autobiographical information. Nevertheless, her extremely popular *Observations and Reflections* came under censure from conservative quarters, which, adhering to the older conventions, found her travel account "a little too trifling and much too egotic." Mrs. Piozzi, as the reviewer points out, wastes too much time relating such details as "where I dined with a prince, where I gave a dinner, where Nardini played a solo, where we wrote the Florence Miscellany, &c."[69]

The role of the travel writer, according to the *Critical Review,* is therefore "to describe the various objects that successively present themselves to his view, to communicate anecdotes of the company he is introduced into, and to relate incidental occurrences that offer themselves to his notice."[70] The relating of a traveler's adventures scarcely falls within his province. He should never play an important role in his own book: "he is rarely discovered to have any excellencies but daring curiosity; he is never the object of admiration, and seldom of esteem." For this reason, men like Bishop Berkeley and Edward Gibbon might include in their private traveling journals all kinds of trivial and autobiographical information that would have to be excised before they would ever think of publishing accounts of their journeys. As the *Monthly Review* points out, a published travel account that adheres too "closely to the form of a journal, or diary" will make "the distance between town and town . . . almost as long and fatiguing to the reader as to the traveller." Sharing this view, Giuseppe Baretti introduces his *Journey from London to Genoa* with an apology for passing too frequently from the proper subject of his travel account to himself. Patrick Brydone's *Tour through Sicily and Malta,* however, very nearly achieves the ideal: as Ralph Griffiths explains, Brydone handles his narrative so well that only "one or two very slight intimations, *en passant,*" enabled readers to guess he was a "governor to some young men of fashion" on the grand tour."[71]

Some eighteenth-century travel writers employed awkward techniques in order to avoid the censure of being too autobiographical. Thomas Pennant, for example, frequently excludes the first-person pronoun from his *Tour in Scotland* (1771). But with the publication of his *Tour in Wales* seven years later, more frequent references to *I* and *me* crept into his writing. Finally, by the time he published his *Journey from Chester to London* in 1782, he fortunately had abandoned this practice. In order to keep from talking about themselves, Arthur Young and William Thomson employ an abbreviated journal style, the latter writer earning the *Critical Review*'s wrath for "dropping the nominative pronoun before the verb, when speaking of himself." According to the reviewer, this "abrupt manner of avoiding egotism . . . is not reconcileable with grammatical accuracy."[72] Other travelers, like Addison and Gilpin, frequently employ the editorial *we;* Ann Radcliffe follows this same practice so frequently in her *Journey* (1795) that she must include a special explanatory note indicating that the *we* refers to herself and her husband, who accompanied her on this trip. "To avoid the language of egotism," Charles Shephard goes so far as to employ *we* when describing actions, reserving *I* only for those instances when he must recount what he observed. Some travelers, like Samuel Derrick and Samuel Ireland, were even driven to substitute *you* for *I* in order to escape the charge of egotism. And Captain Edward Burt was so troubled by the necessity of repeatedly using *I* in his travel account that he censured the English language for lacking the flexibility of

French: "The frequent egotisms which I foresee I shall be obliged to use in passages merely relating to myself, incline me to wish that our language would sometimes (like the French) admit of the third person, only to vary the eternal (I)."[73]

None of these solutions, however, satisfactorily disguises the autobiographical nature of eighteenth-century travel literature. Egotism, explains Samuel Paterson in *Another Traveller!* (1767-1769), must remain the curse of travel writers:

"I said, and I did, and I went"—how shall I get rid of it?—for the soul of me I can't tell!—it hurts myself—how then must it affect my readers?—yet you'll all allow 'tis very difficult for a man to tell a story about himself, and yet to leave himself out of the question.... Of all the writers since the invention of letters, who have endeavoured to entertain the world with talking about themselves, how few have succeeded?[74]

James Edward Smith finds this scarcely a laughing matter. What "may appear like egotism" in his *Sketch of a Tour on the Continent* (1793) arises not from a "fondness for talking of himself, but from his wishing to keep clear of the much more disagreeable appearance of having taken pains to avoid it." In essence, the first-person narrative is an important artistic characteristic of the travel account; with it, the author and the reader are "brought nearer to each other, and the attention of the latter is more strongly excited, than it could have been" through an impersonal relating of facts.[75]

The well-defined subject matter of eighteenth-century travel accounts bears a striking similarity to the kind of information found, if not in autobiographies like Pepys's *Diary*, then certainly in natural histories like Pliny's *Historia naturalis*. As Fielding points out, the travel writer is a commentator on nature.[76] In these terms, little distinguishes a travel book like Edward Burt's *Letters from a Gentleman in the North of Scotland* (1754) from such geographical descriptions as Abbé Lambert's *Collection of Curious Observations* (French 1749; English 1750) and William Borlase's *Natural History of Cornwall* (1758).[77] But while natural histories—what Young would call the "result" of travel—aim primarily at instructing, they are hardly what we would term literature. "In the long catalogue of modern geographical writers," says the *Critical Review,* "we scarce meet with a single name eminent in the Republick of Letters." Moreover, geographical descriptions are arranged according to subject matter rather than the experiences of their authors. Though "founded upon what he himself" had "seen and experienced during two years which he passed on the island," Horrebow's *Natural History of Iceland* (Danish 1752; English 1758) describes Iceland according to various discrete subjects. Such a principle of organization could easily become awkward; Dr. Johnson, for instance, laughingly quoted from memory an entire chapter in Horrebow's book:

> Chapt. LXXII. *Concerning snakes.*
> There are no snakes to be met with throughout the whole island.[78]

An even more unwieldly organization appears in Lambert's *Curious Observations,* which discusses all kinds of subjects "without the least regard to order, and the irreconcileable disparity of the subjects. But this is not all; for if this interweaving of subjects not a little confounds the reader, even when confined to one kingdom or country, must it not quite distract him, when the customs, &c. [of] *China,* for example, are interrupted with an account of *California* or *Peru?*" Even a geography book more regularly organized than Horrebow's would, nevertheless, be what Hawkesworth calls an "index," since it lacks a narrative structure. According to Adam Olearius, a fundamental distinction ultimately separates natural histories from travel accounts. Thus while Smollett initially intended to write "a complete natural history" of Nice and its environs, he finally decided on a travel book, complete with its obligatory framework.[79]

The eighteenth-century travel book is hence a curious blending of its two most frequently cited classical models, Pausanias's *Graeciae descritio* and Horace's "Journey to Brundisium" (Satire I.v). In the marvelously complex frontispiece for his *Travels through Different Cities* (1754), Alexander Drummond places Pausanias's *Description* in the center of all the arts travel writers describe (see fig. 1). The subject matter of Pausanias's work is indeed similar to that of many eighteenth-century travel accounts: it treats "every thing that was

Figure 1. Frontispiece to Alexander Drummond's
*Travels through Different Cities of Germany, Italy, Greece,
and Several Parts of Asia* (London, 1754).

remarkable. All public monuments, as temples, theatres, tombs, statues, paintings, &c. . . . the dimensions of cities . . . [and the] illustrious transactions of old."[80] But though Pausanias's *Description* can appropriately be termed "an account of a journey through Greece," it only rarely refers to his own experiences. Horace's "Journey to Brundisium" more than supplies this lacking autobiographical dimension. "Often imitated by our travelling Bards,"[81] this satire accompanied many English travelers through southern Italy, influencing what they saw and wrote. Though far more personal than any eighteenth-century travel account, Horace's "Journey" clearly influenced the autobiographical form we see in its descendents. Moreover, it seems to have initiated as a literary topos "the infirm traveller," who reappears in the accounts of Fielding, Smollett, and even in a twentieth-century work like Steinbeck's *Travels with Charley,* where the poodle suffers from a prostate condition. But the writer who exclusively employed either Pausanias or Horace as his model, without blending the two, wrote in a form decidedly different from what the eighteenth century considered to be voyages and travels. The account most like Pausanias's was a natural history, while the one most like Horace's was a memoir, usually fictional in nature.

In terms of style, travel accounts aim at "a kind of middle rank between the solidity of studied discourse and the freedom of colloquial conversation." As such, they are usually exempted, in the words of the *Critical Review,* "from the rigid animadversions of criticism."[82] Best suited to the travel account is "a plain unornamented style," one that will impress" on the reader's mind, the fidelity of the relator" without resorting to the jargon of either specialized disciplines or navigational sciences. William Paterson thus proudly proclaims that readers will find "no ornaments of rhetoric" on the pages of his *Narrative of Four Journeys into the Country of the Hottentots* (1789), and Andrew Burnaby studiously avoids "technical or scientific terms" that would give his *Travels through the Middle Settlements in North America* (1775) the appearance of "affectation and pedantry." A humble style indeed tends to argue for the truthfulness of the traveler, the *Monthly Review* asserting that John Macdonald's *Travels, in Various Parts of Europe* (1790) is to be trusted since "no one, capable of inventing, would have assumed so artless and homely a style on the narration." Thus travelers like George Cartwright stress their inability to entertain readers with style and language; fundamental veracity should more than compensate for such superficial deficiencies.[83]

For this reason, many travelers conventionally assert that their accounts were initially intended exclusively either for their own eyes or for the eyes of their friends back at home. Patrick Campbell, perhaps not ingenuously, claims that the journal of his trip into the interior of North America was composed merely for his "own gratification and amusement," its publication coming about only at the insistence of his acquaintances in England. And in a similar vein, Patrick M'Robert explains that the letters that comprise his *Tour through Parts of the North Provinces of America* (1776) "were wrote for the amusement of a particular friend, without the least intention of ever laying them before the publick." Such claims must not be taken too seriously. The Advertisement to *A Tour through Sicily and Malta,* for example, asserts that friends persuaded Patrick Brydone to publish his travel account, a work he originally had intended to be seen only by himself and a few intimates. This Advertisement implies that Brydone's *Tour* appears as it was originally written. We know, however, that William Strahan demanded a considerable amount of stylistic revision, specifically the obliteration of "some Levities, too much in the Shandean Style," before he would publish Brydone's account. In any event, this "persuasion of kind friends," as James Edward Smith calls this common apology at the beginning of travel accounts, can never justify the publication of a truly bad work; it can only set the stylistic tone of sincere plainness and honesty.[84]

The writers who achieve a golden mean between formal discourse and colloquial speech always receive the praise of reviewers, while those who tend toward either a heavy or a conversational style usually face varying degrees of censure. Thus Lettice's *Letters on a Tour through . . . Scotland* (1794) joins pleasure and instruction because its style is "easy and pleasant." By contrast, Dr. Moore's *View of Society and Manners in France* employs a style that "is in many parts loose and careless, sometimes even vulgar," while John Henry

Grose's *Voyage to the East Indies* (1757) is frequently much too "stiff and laboured."[85] A travel book, as a consequence, should instruct without pedantry and entertain without familiarity. But toward the end of the century, more and more travelers cast off the simple elegance of Lady Mary Wortley Montagu's *Letters* (1763), imitating rather the stylistic ease of Mrs. Piozzi's *Observations and Reflections,* which, at least in the eyes of Anna Seward, was "loaded with idioms, debased by vulgarnesses," and marred "by chamber-maid flippancy."[86]

The century saw travel literature, therefore, as "Science . . . connected with Events." As "Science," it is closely akin to treatises on geography: as "Events," it bears a striking similarity to autobiography.[87] Ideally, the author carefully weighed these two concerns in favor of science. But as the century progressed, many travel books focused more on events and less on its former partner. To an extent, this gradual change reflects the growing technical nature of science: no longer could the knowledgeable gentleman be master of all natural and experimental sciences. In addition, this change reflects the widening rift between pleasure and instruction as the joint aims of literature. But as we shall see in the next two chapters, the gradual transformation of eighteenth-century travel literature also results from attempts to correct the abuses of previous travel writers, from the influence of works like Sterne's *Sentimental Journey,* and from experimentation with increasingly difficult descriptive techniques.

# II

## NARRATIVE CONVENTIONS IN EIGHTEENTH-CENTURY NONFICTION TRAVEL LITERATURE

---

> A pompous book must show,
> What much it must concern the world to know;
> How far they walk'd — where halted — din'd and slept;
> What inns — good meat — good wine — good lodgings kept;
> What dangers, what fatigues they underwent,
> And wore their shoes out — and their money spent.
> — Thomas Beck, *The Age of Frivolity* (1806)

Many early eighteenth-century travel books, like Defoe's *Tour thro' the Whole Island of Great Britain,* contain only the barest hint of a narrative sequence. Defoe introduces his description of Tunbridge-Wells, for instance, simply by explaining that it would not be foreign to his design, after viewing the great iron works of Kent and Sussex, if he refreshed himself "with a view of Tunbridge-Wells, which were not then above twelve miles" out of his way.[1] Upon arriving at the resort, he reports encountering "a great deal of good company," which made lodgings difficult to find. But in describing the Wells, he ignores his own particular experiences except to speak of seeing a turbot weighing nearly twenty pounds. He does not mention his dates of arrival and departure, nor does he describe lodgings, acquaintances, or daily perambulations about the city. Yet upon completing his description of Tunbridge-Wells, Defoe resumes the sort of personal narrative he had temporarily abandoned by explaining why he traveled to still another place:

I left Tunbridge, for the same reason that I give, why others should leave it, when they are in my condition; namely, that I found my money almost

47

gone; and tho' I had bills of credit to supply my self in the course of my intended journey; yet I had none there; so I came away, or as they call it
there, I retir'd; and came to Lewes, through the deepest, dirtiest, but many
ways the richest, and most profitable country in all that part of England.

Defoe may well have invented this sequence of events; by juxtapos-
ing descriptions of industry and farming with pictures of the frivo-
lous life at a fashionable watering place, he interjects contrast and
variety into his book. And perhaps he reports spending most of his
money at the resort not because it actually happened, but because it
was a customary practice of visitors there. In any case, Defoe's narrative surfaces only occasionally, never directing the reader's attention away from the geographical subject of *A Tour*. Though it gives
balance and order to his descriptions, it never hints at being part of
a fictional plot, and hence it never casts doubt on the basically truthful nature of the travel account.

   This minimal use of autobiography in *A Tour* rests firmly on Defoe's understanding of the rules for writing travel literature. In
introducing the third volume of his *Tour*, he specifically censures
the kind of traveler who "takes up his own time, or his reader's
pateince, in observing trifles" concerning insignificant autobiographical experiences. To support this attack, Defoe relates a para-
ble about two gentlemen who journeyed together through most of
England:

   The result of their observations were very different indeed; one of them
took some minutes of things for his own satisfaction, but not much; but the
other, as he said, took an exact journal; the case was thus:
   He that took minutes only, those minutes were very critical, and upon
some very significant things; but for the rest his memory was so good, and
he took so good notice of every thing worth observing, that he wrote a very
good and useful account of his whole journey after his return....
   The other gentleman's papers, which I called an exact journal, contained the following very significant heads:
   I.    The day of the month when he set out.
   II.   The names of the towns where they din'd every day, and where they
         lodg'd at night.
   III.  The signs of the inns where they din'd and lodg'd, with the memo-
         randums of which had good claret, which not.

IV. The day of the month when he return'd.

The moral of this brief story, which I insist that I know to be true, is very much to my purpose. The difference between these two gentlemen in their travelling, and in their remarks upon their journey, is a good emblem of the differing genius in readers, as well as authors, and may be a guide to both in the work now before us.

Defoe carefully attempts to avoid such trifles in his *Tour*. If his book on that account is "too grave for some people," it nevertheless should please those who are interested in "the advancement and encrease of knowledge." But unwilling to forgo the recognized objectives of pleasure and instruction, he hopes his *Tour* will make readers both "wise" and "merry" even though it does not describe the signs of inns and the merits of various clarets.

In trusting that his *Tour* will not be too grave because he has omitted trifles, Defoe recognizes the entertainment value of a properly handled narrative while at the same time he attacks the "exact journal" as being too autobiographical. As Hawkesworth says, "No species of writing affords so general entertainment, as the relation of events." Hence, according to Samuel Ireland, the introduction of events into a travel account provides "some variation to a work that, to the general eye, may be thought to stand in need of extraneous relief."[2] Like Thomson's *Seasons,* travel accounts threaten to become dull description with no action, and unless rescued by at least a sketchy narrative, they invite objections similar to those that Swift and Johnson pronounced on Thomson's poem, which inevitably lacks "order," "suspense," and "expectation." But while avoiding this danger, the travel writer throughout most of the century must be extremely selective in his choice of incidents; unless careful, he will either, with puerile exactness, lapse into recording the trivial occurrences of each day or, with dishonest feigning, spin out a tale that appears fictional to his readers.[3]

In order to avoid the dullness of sheer description, some travel accounts resort to elaborately developed anecdotes that appear basically autobiographical in form. Paying lip service to travel-book conventions, Smollett claims that his personal adventures on the road do not bear recital. But despite this declaration, he immediately turns his *Travels through France and Italy* into a detailed nar-

rative of "petty disputes with landladies, postmasters, and postilions" at Sens:

My servant, who had rode on before to bespeak fresh horses, told me, that
the domestic of another company had been provided before him, although
it was not his turn, as he had arrived later at the post. Provoked at this par-
tiality, I resolved to chide the postmaster, and accordingly addressed myself to a person who stood at the door of the auberge. He was a jolly figure,
fat and fair, dressed in an odd kind of garb, with a gold-laced cap on his
head, and a cambric handkerchief pinned to his middle. The sight of such
a fantastic *petit-maître* in the character of a postmaster increased my
spleen. I called to him with an air of authority, mixed with indignation,
and when he came up to the coach, asked in a peremptory tone, if he did
not understand the king's ordonnance concerning the regulation of the
posts? He laid his hand upon his breast; but before he could make any
answer, I pulled out the post-book, and began to read with great vocifera-
tion the article which orders that the traveller who comes first shall be first
served. By this time the fresh horses being put to the carriage, and the
postilions mounted, the coach set off all of a sudden with uncommon
speed. I imagined the postmaster had given the fellows a signal to be gone,
and, in this persuasion, thrusting my head out at the window, I bestowed
some epithets upon him, which must have sounded very harsh in the ears of
a Frenchman. We stopped for a refreshment at a little town called Joigne-
ville, where, by the bye, I was scandalously imposed upon, and even abused
by a virago of a landlady; then proceeding to the next stage I was given to
understand we could not be supplied with fresh horses. Here I perceived at
the door of the inn the same person whom I had reproached at Sens. He
came up to the coach, and told me, that notwithstanding what the guides
had said, I should have fresh horses in a few minutes. I imagined he was
master both of this house and the auberge at Sens, between which he passed
and repassed occasionally; and that he was now desirous of making me
amends for the affront he had put upon me at the other place. Observing
that one of the trunks behind was a little displaced, he assisted my servant
in adjusting it: then he entered into conversation with me, and gave me to
understand, that in a post-chaise, which we had passed, was an English
gentleman on his return from Italy. I wanted to know who he was, and
when he said he could not tell, I asked him, in a very abrupt manner, why
he had not inquired of his servant? He shrugged up his shoulders and re-
tired to the inn door. Having waited above half an hour, I beckoned to
him, and when he approached, upbraided him with having told me that I

should be supplied with fresh horses in a few minutes. He seemed shocked, and answered, that he thought he had reason for what he had said, observing, that it was as disagreeable to him as to me to wait for a relay. As it began to rain, I pulled up the glass in his face, and he withdrew again to the door, seemingly ruffled at my deportment. In a little time the horses arrived, and three of them were immediately put to a very handsome post-chaise, into which he stepped, and set out, accompanied by a man in a rich livery on horse-back. Astonished at this circumstance, I asked the ostler who he was, and he replied that he was a man of fashion, un seigneur, who lived in the neighbourhood of Auxerre, I was much mortified to find that I had treated a nobleman so scurvily.[4]

In this humorous story, Smollett the travel writer becomes Smollett the novelist. In an entertaining diversion in the midst of his factual subject matter, he carefully develops suspense so that readers begin wondering about the odd-looking "postmaster" in the third sentence and do not learn his real identity until the conclusion. No longer an observer of "Character, Customs, Religion, Government, Police, Commerce, Arts and Antiquities" of France and Italy,[5] Smollett here becomes, at least for the time being, the center of interest in his book.

Henry Fielding also manipulates the narrative portions of his travel account in order to provide *The Journal of a Voyage to Lisbon* with a little humor and suspense. Recounting his experiences with Mrs. Francis, his hostess on the Isle of Ryde, Fielding explains that she differed "in every particular from her husband; but very remarkably in this, that as it was impossible to displease him, so it was impossible to please her; and as no art could remove a smile from his countenance, so could no art carry it into hers."[6] A continual battle raged between Fielding and this shrew: they fought about food, prices, and the proper conduct of innkeepers. One of their first arguments arose over her preparations for Fielding's traveling party. Mrs. Francis, as Fielding expalins, had "no sooner received news of our intended arrival, than she considered more the gentility, than the humanity of her guests, and applied herself not to that which kindles, but to that which extinguishes fire, and forgetting to put on her pot, fell to washing her house." While most travelers would have considered house cleaning a proper preparation for new lodgers,

Fielding, who suffered from severe dropsy, scarcely felt this the case. He consequently complained loudly about "sitting in a damp room . . . which was by no means to be neglected in a valetudinary state." To remedy this situation, Mrs. Fielding searched through the entire inn, finding only one place "which had escaped the mop. . . . This was a dry, warm, oaken floored barn, lined on both sides with wheaten straw, and opening at one end into a green field, and a beautiful prospect."[7] Fielding's comic preference for Mrs. Francis's barn over her inn naturally overshadows, at least for the time being, the descriptive objectives of his travel book. One of Fielding's eighteenth-century publishers indeed capitalized precisely on this narrative, choosing a picture of the meal in Mrs. Francis's barn to serve as the frontispiece for his edition of the *Voyage to Lisbon* (see fig. 2). But unlike Smollett, whose novelist's imagination understandably enhanced his account of what is probably an actual event, Fielding seems entirely to have fabricated this comic incident. Writing to Samuel Richardson, Jane Collier describes the real Mrs. Francis, whose plight should have raised nothing but the traveler's compassion:

She was naturally afflicted with too much gall, and now indeed was plainly dying under the overflowing of it, and consequently demanded great allowances on that score; but I am surprized that so great an observer of the humours of the lower class of people, had never discovered that the circumstances of paying them, will not always make them amends for the trouble you give them.

Moreover, Miss Collier discovered that the whole episode involving Fielding's meal in the barn was a fiction, since even the barn, with its supposedly pleasant view, never existed except in Fielding's imagination.[8] Mr. and Mrs. Francis in fact seem but refurbished versions of Mr. and Mrs. Tow-wouse, who had appeared some dozen years earlier in *Joseph Andrews*. Mr. Tow-wouse, like Mr. Francis, is a good-natured innkeeper. He kindly cares for the waylaid Joseph just as Mr. Francis looks after the ill Fielding, and both hostelers turn over to their wives the running of their businesses. The women, in direct contrast to their husbands, are selfish, unloving, and ill natured, more concerned with making money than performing

Figure 2. Michael Angelo Rooker's frontispiece to
Vol. XII of *The Works of Henry Fielding, Esq.*,
new ed. (London, 1783).

good deeds. Thus, contrary to Fielding's statements, Mr. and Mrs. Francis are more like exaggerated caricatures than real people. No wonder that the *Gentleman's Magazine* specifically singled out Fielding's description of these two "originals" as examples of that kind of humor in which he "excelled every other writer of his age."[9]

Occasionally travel writers become carried away with the narrative portions of their books. In the first version of his *View of Society and Manners in France,* for example, Dr. John Moore carefully modeled his opening narrative after the epistolary technique of *Humphry Clinker,* which next to Sterne's *Sentimental Journey* was the most popular fictionalized travel account of the second half of the century. Explaining in his first two letters that he has been impoverished by an addiction to gambling, Moore recounts his appeals to various people who owe him money but who repay him with only "some sad tale of an unforeseen accident." He then describes his vain attempts to persuade one of his old companions in London to give up gambling. Thinking it "most prudent to remove beyond the influence" of his old acquaintances, Moore next sells his house in London and travels to Paris, where, as he says, "I . . . am fully convinced that I can live within my remaining yearly income with more satisfaction than I enjoyed when I spent five times that sum" in London. Persevering in this plan, Moore believes he will be able to clear "all incumbrances within a few years."[10] The similarities with *Humphry Clinker* are obvious. Like Matthew Bramble, who journeys to the Hot Wells at Bristol for the sake of his health, Moore sets out for Europe in order to mend his finances. Bramble initially speaks of the "ridiculous incident that happened . . . to my niece Liddy," and Moore describes the disastrous occurrences at the gambling table. Both men reveal they are fundamentally good-natured, Bramble giving instructions to sell his corn to the poor at a shilling a bushel under market price, and Moore attempting to save a fellow gambler from ruining himself. Hence the opening letter in each case seems to define an unstable situation, the resolution of which will form a fictional plot.

This admiring imitation of *Humphry Clinker* unfortunately created a mixture of narrative and descriptive forms that badly confused the recognized generic objectives of travel literature. By picturing himself as a reformed rake who deserves the sympathy of his reader, Moore creates narrative suspense: Will the author success-fully mend his fortune? Can he avoid the temptations of the gam-bling table? Yet simultaneously, Moore strives to arouse the reader's curiosity concerning what the reformed gambler sees during his travels. Thus in addressing his "correspondent," Moore says:

> You insist so much on my writing to you regularly, from the different places where I may reside during my absence from England, that I begin to believe you are in earnest, and shall certainly obey your commands.
> I know you do not expect from me a minute account of churches....
> The manners, customs, and characters of the people may probably furnish the chief materials, in the correspondence you exact, with such reflections as may arise from the subject.[11]

While this promised descriptive information is typical of many ear-lier travel books, the narrative itself would have been suitable only in a fictional work.

Moore's promise to supply the "manners and customs" expected of a travel book could not, however, save his *View* from censure. According to the *Critical Review*, Moore resorted in his opening pages to a narrative that unfortunately "has too much the air of a novel."[12] Taking this criticism seriously, Moore carefully revised his second edition by diminishing its fictional appearance. As his new Advertisement explains:

> From a diffidence of his own abilities, and from other motives not so well founded, the Author of the following Letters thought it expedient, in the First Edition, to throw a slight veil over the real situation in which they were written.... But having been assured by those of whose friendship and judgment he is equally convinced, that the assumed character and feigned situation in the two first letters gave an *air of fiction* to the real incidents in the rest of the work, he has now restored those two letters to their original form.[13]

In this new edition, the reformed gambler remains, but now simply in the guise of one of Moore's passing acquaintances, not the author himself. Slight though it might seem, this alteration completely changes the form of the entire book. *A View* no longer appears, if only momentarily, to be an epistolary novel. The traveler journeys through Europe in order to describe "manners, customs, and characters" for inclusion in his travel account, while the reformed rake remains in London in order to mend his fortune and is never heard of again. Suspense concerning relapse or reformation no longer colors the book as a whole, the incident concerning the gambler now serving merely as one of several entertaining narrative digressions. Moore's *View* thus becomes similar to Fielding's *Voyage to Lisbon:* while both works may contain fictional anecdotes, these departures from truth do not obscure the basically nonfictional form of the travel accounts.

While the narrative in a travel book usually provided a kind of entertainment, it could easily cause problems when it blurred distinctions between fiction and nonfiction. For example, one reviewer could not make up his mind whether *The Voyages and Adventures of the Chevalier Dupont* (French 1769; English 1772) related true experiences and presented accurate descriptions of foreign countries. Although he classified Dupont's *Voyages* as a novel because it contained so many adventures, he nevertheless recognized that its incidents, like those in authentic travel accounts, were neither romantic nor extraordinary. In a similar fashion, *Letters to an Officer, Stationed at an Interior Post in North America* (1773) perplexed yet another reviewer because, even if the reported events were true, they were so "embellished as to wear the appearance of Novels." And the *Critical Review* likewise questioned whether Captain John Smith's travel tales, which "savour strongly of romance," should be included in Derrick's *Collection of Travels* (1762). Behind all such questionings stands the nagging suspicion that travelers by their very nature are apt to stretch the truth in order to entertain their audiences. "It is a common Saying, and indeed generally proves true," complained Daniel Beeckman toward the beginning of the century, "*That Old Men and Travellers do give themselves great Liberty in relating fictitious and improbable Stories.*"[14]

Because of such uncertainties, readers during most of the eighteenth century tended to doubt the authenticity of a traveler's descriptions whenever his narrative appeared even slightly fictional. In attacking a travel writer who assumed a feigned character, Dr. Johnson pointed out that many other lies may remain hidden in his book.[15] Thus when Pierre Jean Grosley rather innocently pretended to be a native of Sweden in his *New Observations on Italy* (French 1764; English 1769), his pretense did not escape the censure of the reviewers.[16] Though they may seem extreme today, these reactions were natural enough to an age that had been gulled by Psalmanazars and Patagonian giants. For a while, George Psalmanazar convinced London society that he was a native of Formosa. His anecdotes and ultimately his *Historical and Geographical Description of Formosa* (1704) paint a romantic picture of that faraway paradise where inhabitants customarily eat raw meat and where on each New Year's Day they offer human sacrifices. Despite a series of pamphlet attacks and Psalmanazar's admission that he was born in France, his *Description of Formosa* nevertheless managed to find its way into at least one nineteenth-century catalog of authentic travel descriptions.[17] The supposed existence of Patagonian giants, perhaps dating back to Antonio Pigafetta's sixteenth-century journal, misled even more Englishmen. As late in the century as 1767, the *Critical Review* felt that the reality of these giants had been "confirmed" by *A Voyage round the World, in the Years 1764-66, in His Majesty's Sloop the Dolphin*, which "has the air of being a real journal."[18] This imposition on readers, lasting almost two and a half centuries, effectively ceased only when Hawkesworth published the accurate measurements—interesting though unspectacular—of the "giants" in his *Account of the Voyages*.[19]

Because of such impostures, travel accounts, especially those describing faraway places, frequently inspired an unmerited distrust among eighteenth-century readers. "Many relations of travellers," as Dr. Johnson explains in *Idler* 87, "have been slighted as fabulous, till more frequent voyages have confirmed their veracity." But even Johnson could misjudge travel tales on the basis of their seeming absurdity. One cannot, after all, always distinguish between truth and falsity solely on the grounds of apparent realism. James Bruce, after traveling through Abyssinia in search of the Nile's headwaters, greeted London in 1774 with numerous anecdotes that he spread while writing an account of his travels. Among his seemingly prepos-

terous stories was a tale about how he, following the normal Abys-
sinian custom, had eaten raw meat cut from live cows. This story—
incidentally much like the one told by Psalmanazar about the eating habits of the Formosans—earned Bruce the derision of many of
his contemporaries, including Dr. Johnson, who was considered an
expert on Abyssinia because of his translation of Father Lobo's *Voyage historique d'Abissinie* and his own *Rasselas, Prince of Abissinia*.
Burlesqued as Macfable on the stage, attacked by Peter Pindar's
doggerel, and satirized in Raspe's *Adventures of Baron Munchausen*
(1785), Bruce became the laughing stock of much of London.[20] Ultimately, such tales led at least some readers to doubt whether he had
ever seen Abyssinia at all.[21] Only subsequent travelers, most notably
Dr. Edward Clarke at the beginning of the nineteenth century, were
able to rescue Bruce's reputation by substantiating his descriptions
of that remote country. Bruce's problem resulted from his failure to
follow a well-established rule for travelers: "It is not sufficient to
write things true, but they must likewise seem probable, to gain
belief."[22]

    While travelers like Johnson, Young, and Martyn could rely on
their reputations as truthful men,[23] less well-known writers had to
resort to other means to attest to their veracity. Appended statements, frequently little more than unreliable puffs, often take the
form of Henry Swinburne's opening plea in his *Travels through
Spain* (1779):

There is but one merit I insist upon, that of a steady adherence to Veracity,
as far as I was able to discern Truth from Falsehood. I may be detected in
many mistakes; because a foreigner must often be exposed to receive par-
tial accounts of things from the natives, who have an interest in hiding the
nakedness of their country, and in exaggerating its advantages; but I shall
never be detected in a wilful perversion of the truth.

When such testimonies are written by translators, editors, or publishers, they tend to become even more hyperbolic, like the description of Van Egmond and Heyman at the beginning of their *Travels
through Part of Europe* (Dutch 1757-1758; English 1759):

It is...no wonder, that persons of the greatest learning and wisdom,
have, in all ages, been excited to visit foreign countries, in order to enquire

into the wonderful productions of nature and art, and make themselves acquainted with the customs and manners of the inhabitants. To acquire this they have disregarded fatigue and expence; nay even hazarded their lives in order to improve their minds. . . .

Among these useful members of society we may justly reckon those two eminent persons, whose travels we now present to the publick. A work long desired by many learned and respectable members of the university of Leyden, who after perusing the manuscripts were pleased to express their approbation of them in terms that do honour to the authors.[24]

Little trust, however, can be placed in such puffery. While Swinburne, Van Egmond, and Heyman seem to have been honest travelers, dishonest ones frequently employed this same kind of statement in an attempt, sometimes successful, to cover over their lies. For instance, the *Critical Review,* in a clearly uncritical moment, fell victim to the French Editor's Preface and the Preface by the Translator at the beginning of *The Shipwreck and Adventures of Mons. Pierre Viaud* (French 1770; English 1771). Proclaiming that these so-called authentic certificates sufficiently prove the truthfulness of M. Viaud's account, the reviewer failed to recognize the obviously fictional format of this work.[25] Such certificates had long been a tradition in travel literature when Swift poked fun at them at the beginning of *Gulliver's Travels,* where the "publisher" attests to Gulliver's veracity, showing that it had become "a sort of Proverb among his Neighbors at *Redriff,* when any one affirmed a Thing, to say, it was as true as if Mr. *Gulliver* had spoke it."

Having no other relatively reliable means of verifying the truthfulness of an unknown author, eighteenth-century readers necessarily judged the veracity of a travel book on the basis of its adherence to the recognized conventions of travel literature. "Internal evidence," for example, convinces "every Reader" that the anonymous *Journal of a Voyage round the World, in His Majesty's Ship Endeavour* (1771) is in fact authentic.[26] Authors could, of course, trick readers and reviewers alike. While the *Monthly Review* seems to have judged *A Journal of a Voyage . . . in His Majesty's Ship Endeavour* perceptively, it later incorrectly decided—as did the *Critical Review*—that on the basis of internal evidence, Joseph Marshall's *Travels through Holland, Flanders . . . and Poland* (1772) was a genuine account, its author "a man of veracity" who had contributed "both to the amusement of his readers, and the improvement of his country." In this case, "internal evidence" unfortunately only meant a similarity to descriptions in other travel accounts, a criterion that was necessarily bound to fail. The high praise for Marshall's *Travels* thus rapidly turned sour when a correspondent informed the *Monthly Review* that Joseph Marshall was a fictitious person and that his book, like *The Travels of the Late Charles Thompson* (1744), was simply a compilation of previously published travel accounts.[27]

Such spurious accounts, written by persons who never traveled outside the city limits of London, plagued the eighteenth-century reader. Dr. Syntax's mercenary bookdealer could scarcely have been unique in his boasts:

> We can get Tours—don't make wry faces,
> From those who never saw the places!
> I know a man who has the skill
> To make you Books of Tours at will;
> And from his garret in Moorfields
> Can see what ev'ry country yields.[28]

Like this bookdealer's man, many an eighteenth-century hack eked out a few pounds for writing a bogus tour made up of materials stolen from authentic travel and geography books. The penniless stutterer in *Humphry Clinker* is one such author, who could narrate "his travels through Europe and part of Asia, without ever budging beyond the liberties of the King's Bench, except in term-time, with a tipstaff for his companion." Even the pompous account at the beginning of John Northall's *Travels through Italy* (1766) did not fool the *Critical Review* into believing that its author had ever quitted "his elbow-chair or his fire-side." Sarcastically recommending Northall's *Travels* as "one of the most judicious and useful compilations," the reviewer suggests that Northall may well be a relative of Charles Thompson, "who travelled through half the globe, without stirring out of the sound of Bow-Bell."[29] Fireside travels, in spite of such attacks, must have been relatively popular—and therefore profitable—since they not infrequently provided, as one reviewer indicated, more entertainment than authentic accounts.[30] Indeed, Charles Thompson's *Travels* went through at least five printings in the eighteenth century and one in the nineteenth. But reviewers usually looked for convincing evidence in a travel account that would indicate that its writer had crossed the seas.[31] As a consequence, Joseph Cradock's *Letters from Snowdon* (1770) received, quite unjustly, John Langhorne's censure for seeming "a mere piece of authorism, consisting of anecdotes and descriptions, which any industrious compiler might pick up and give us, either from the top of Snowdon, or from an ale-house at the bottom, or from a garret in Field-Lane."[32] Titles like *Tour thro' Britain* and *Voyage round the World,* as Archibald Campbell points out, do not necessarily indicate that an author ever left the confines of London. Indeed, the writer profits from staying in his garret since he can finish his book more quickly and with less expense than a genuine traveler.[33]

Duped by such fireside travelers, readers often suspected the accounts of genuine travelers. In 1704 Awnsham and John Churchill confidently included Giovanni Francesco Gemelli Careri's *Giro del mondo* (1699-1700) in their *Collection of Voyages and Travels.*[34] But when readers discovered striking similarities between his *Giro* and previously published accounts, his reputation rapidly dwindled. By 1761 Goldsmith could assert in *Citizen of the World* Letter 108 that "the learned" had long agreed Gemelli's book was simply an imposture, and at the end of the century Gemelli served as a prime example in the *Critical Review* of the kind of author who must be classified as "a compiler rather than a traveller."[35] Nevertheless, as subsequent scholarship has shown, Gemelli scarcely deserved this reputation as a fireside traveler. The damning similarities only indicate that he followed a well-beaten path in his travels and that in some instances he augmented his book with facts taken from earlier writers in an attempt to make his account more nearly complete.[36]

Though Gemelli's reputation as an unreliable traveler dates at least as far back as 1735,[37] one would expect that his status should have been bolstered with the publication of his *Giro* in Smollett's *Compendium of Authentic and Entertaining Voyages* (1756). But in abridging Gemelli's account, Smollett omitted most of the anecdotes that had enlivened both the original Italian version and its English translation.[38] By so doing, he effectively removed from Gemelli's account the narrative portion, that part serving as the clearest indication that Gemelli's descriptions are based on his own experiences. The *Critical Review,* for instance, would have judged *Observations on the Manners and Customs of Italy* (1798) a mere compilation had it not contained "some intrinsic evidence, that the author had really been in Italy."[39] Removing such intrinsic evidence from Gemelli's account, Smollett casts even further doubt upon the traveler whom he quotes.

Recognition of similarity between two travel accounts does not, in itself, prove that one traveler plagiarized from another, unless, of course, both employ identical phraseology. In describing cities, buildings, natural settings, customs, and the like, a degree of similarity in fact strengthens the credibility of both works: if they do not agree in their most basic descriptions of a place like Venice, the reader inevitably suspects that at least one of the travelers is inaccurate, if not dishonest. Scientists like Samuel Stanhope Smith, who invariably distrusted the first descriptions of any place, demanded a concurrence between several travel accounts before crediting any treatment of faraway countries.[40] Travelers, especially those touring the Continent, frequently described cities in a similar order, often picking out identical sights in each city to criticize and discuss. This practice ultimately dictated obligatory routes to be followed and sights to be seen for the eighteenth-century gentleman on his grand tour. In examining Italy, for example, the traveler followed one of several standard routes.[41] Addison, aside from leaving the beaten track to view San Marino, violated convention only in that he traveled through Italy in reverse order, going first to Venice rather than Florence. A visit to particular buildings like the Ambrosian Library in Milan and to natural curiosities like the Grotto del Cani near Naples became *de rigueur* for the fashionable Englishman, with descriptions of these places consequently finding their way into most English travel accounts. By the end of the century often-reprinted guides like Nugent's *Grand Tour* and Millard's *Gentleman's Guide* firmly standardized paths through Europe and sights to be seen along these paths.

But while two travelers might well describe Venice in similar terms, and while their routes leading to it might easily have been the same, their particular experiences on the road and in the city were expected to differ. For this reason, the narrative portion of a travel account serves eighteenth-century readers as a frequent, if fallible, proof that the traveler actualy visited the places he describes. Most detectable "fireside travellers" chose one of two tactics to disguise their fraud. Some, like Countess d'Aulnoy, concocted involved, fictional stories that often give their books the formal appearance of novels. But more frequently, like Charles Thompson, they virtually omitted all narrative details, causing their works to look much like natural histories or guide books.

Thus, the eighteenth-century travel writer tried to achieve a "golden mean": he had to include a sufficiently detailed record of his experiences to prove that he actually visited the countries he described, but he could not tell too much about himself and his adventures. If his narrative appeared too circumstantial, he would usually be attacked as an egotist; if it seemed too contrived, he would frequently be criticized as a writer of fiction, primarily interested in entertaining readers at the expense of their instruction. A properly handled narrative, therefore, not only provides entertainment but also certifies the truthfulness of the book. While some travel writers, especially toward the end of the century, willingly sacrifice truthfulness for increased entertainment, they ideally give readers a judicious mixture of honesty and pleasure. According to the *Critical Review*, French travelers habitually ignore this important balance, for they "always invent and embellish" their narratives. Such is the perversity of a "careless reader" who, preferring "a boasting romancer" to an honest traveler, makes these accounts, in the words of the reviewer, "the most popular even among us." Yet in trying to turn the tide of romantic travels, Mungo Park's *Travels in the Interior Districts of Africa* (1799), like William Browne's *Travels in Africa, Egypt, and Syria* (1799), earned the *Critical Review*'s special praise for the manner in which they describe "events as they occurred." The truthful nature of these works by no means hinders their ability to entertain.[42]

As might be expected, reviewers paid special attention to narrative details when assessing the validity of travel books. The absence of autobiographical material caused the *Monthly Review* to suspect that Alexander Cluny's *American Traveller* (1769) was an imposture, its information simply "brought into one point of view from the many accounts already published of our settlements, by an experienced compiler."[43] Indeed, while most of Lord Baltimore's *Tour to the East* contains both a narrative of his experiences and a description of the countries he visited, the last part of the book, according to the *Critical Review,* "is almost totally unembellished by any description, and therefore carries with it the most evident marks of truth." As this reviewer's argument apparently runs, descriptions can be gleaned from other travel books, but a narrative of experiences in foreign countries can be constructed only from real life. Even though this part of Baltimore's work fails to maintain an ideal balance between narration and description, it nonetheless avoids the censure of "egotism." According to the *Critical Review,* the public may rely upon Baltimore's "veracity for whatever he advances," and though he spends much of the concluding part of his *Tour* relating his own experiences, he never "touched at Rhodes; for no author can be more free than his lordship is, from Rhodomontades."[44] Using these same principles, the *Monthly Review* doubted the accuracy of *Observations on the Religion, Laws, Government, and Manners of the Turks* (1768), since its author omitted the kind of narrative that would attest to his actual residence in Turkey.[45] These "observations" earned respect only when Sir James Porter identified himself as the author, his position as British ambassador at Constantinople assuring readers that his descriptions derived from firsthand experience.

Even a well-balanced and convincing narrative, however, did not always earn the trust of eighteenth-century readers. Though "Lying Travellers" could sometimes be recognized by these means, "Idle Travellers" still remained to be dealt with.[46] Like Goldoni's trunk, many an eighteenth-century gentleman found himself bounced from carriage to carriage, conveyed from one town to another, and then returned home improved merely by a thick cover of dust and a number of scratches collected along the way.[47] Because such travelers usually were inattentive, they remained chronically uninformed when composing accounts, and they could therefore lead a reader as far afield as the liar could. The twentieth century scarcely has a monopoly on whirlwind or careless tourists. "The greater part of travellers," according to Dr. Johnson,

tell nothing, because their method of travelling supplies them with nothing to be told. He that enters a town at night and surveys it in the morning, and then hastens away to another place, and guesses at the manners of the inhabitants by the entertainment which his inn afforded him, may please himself for a time . . . but let him be contented to please himself without endeavouring to disturb others.[48]

Laurence Sterne, ridiculing such travelers who presume to describe accurately cities and countries after brief stays, has Tristram remark, upon leaving Chantilly:

—No;—I cannot stop a moment to give you the character of the people —their genius—their manners—their customs—their laws—their religion —their government—their manufactures—their commerce—their finances, with all the resources and hidden springs which sustain them: qualified as I may be, by spending three days and two nights amongst them, and during all that time, making these things the entire subject of my enquiries and reflections.
Still—still I must away.

Samuel Paterson similarly attacks whirlwind tourists in *Another Traveller!,* where Coriat Junior describes Bruges in the following manner:

I tell you very fairly that my time was so short that I saw but little of that once flourishing city, arriving there only in the evening, and leaving it by nine o'clock the next morning; so that it was with the utmost difficulty in so large a place, that I made shift to run up one street and down another—to pop my head first into one church, then into another—If any of the courteous inhabitants did me the honour of a salute *en passant,* as is very customary; to present them with my best bows in return—to step into one shop, and ask for snuff; and into another to buy a memorandum-book, with the better grace to inform myself of the name of such a place, or such an edifice.

" 'Tis fine," Coriat sarcastically remarks, to talk "of seeing *every thing* in three or four days in such a capital as *Brussels,* and being

acquainted with the people into the bargain!—Commend me to
such ingrossers of curiosity!"[49] Many a traveler, according to
Thomas Cogan, would have hurried his coach through Paradise
itself just to reach the next town on his itinerary with some degree of
comfort.[50] Arthur Young, not surprisingly, censures in the same
breath both fireside travelers and those who describe foreign countries after whirling their ways through Europe in post chaises.[51] Neither writer, according to the author of *Travels in France,* has the
knowledge necessary for composing a travel account.

Perhaps Young learned this lesson from his own mistakes. At least
two reviewers attacked him for not stopping "long enough to be
accurately and perfectly informed of the facts he asserts" in *A Six
Weeks' Tour through the Southern Counties of England and Wales*
(1768). Two years later Ralph Griffiths emphatically advised him,
while reviewing his *Six Months Tour through the North of England,*
not to travel too fast when trying to write about his next trip.[52] By
the time *A Farmer's Tour through the East of England* (1771)
appeared, such criticism had disappeared. Titles of his subsequent
works indeed stress the length of time he devoted to his travels: *A
Tour in Ireland* (1780) contains, as its title page indicates, observations "Made in the Years 1776, 1777, and 1778. And Brought Down
to the End of 1779," and his last travel account bears the unwieldy
title of *Travels during the Years 1787, 1788 and 1789, Undertaken
More Particularly with a View of Ascertaining the Cultivation,
Wealth, Resources, and National Prosperity, of the Kingdom of
France.*

Reviewers frequently singled out for special censure travelers who
tried to describe foreign countries after virtually whirling their ways
through country lanes and city streets. Because of his *Nouveaux
memoires, ou observations sur l'Italie,* translated into English by
Thomas Nugent in 1769, Pierre Jean Grosley had quickly become a
respected travel writer, his book superseding Misson's as the *vade
mecum* for the Frenchman in Italy. But English readers of Grosley's
*Tour to London* (French 1770; English 1772) delighted in pointing
out his numerous silly mistakes, the result of a speedy glance at their
country. On his first excursion through London, as the *Critical*

*Review* points out, Grosley accurately observes "that the Thames is not adorned with quays like the Seine, but that the houses are built close to the river." But he then outrageously attributes this difference between London and Paris to the natural bent for suicide among Englishmen, who are protected from self-destruction in this fashion. In order to drown themselves, they must leave the confines of the city, "but the length of the way thither, and the consequent opportunity of reflecting, are circumstances most likely to prevent such mischief." Reviewers could only laugh at such misconceptions, pointing out "how vain it is for a person, even of the greatest abilities, to attain, in the space of a few weeks, that knowledge of men and manners, which demands the study of years." As Jebez Hirons indicates, Grosley simply "did not continue in England a sufficient time to collect his materials, or form his opinions and strictures with that deliberation and precision which are requisite in order to make a fair and judicious report of the state and manners of a people." Thanks to his *Tour to London,* Grosley's reputation suffered enormously, with at least one reviewer suspecting that Grosley may, after all, have committed as many errors in his formerly respected *New Observations on Italy.*[53]

Many travel writers understandably tried to avoid such accusations of haste. Some, like Henry Swinburne, included introductory statements attesting to their competence as deliberate and careful observers. Not "under any restraint in point of time," Swinburne asserts that he did not rush from place to place as did many previous writers who "had neither time nor opportunity to procure much information" concerning Spain.[54] Others, like William Dalrymple, employ epigrams on their title pages, indicating that they traveled slowly and hence observed accurately. "The Characters of Nature are legible," says Dalrymple quoting Burke at the beginning of *Travels through Spain and Portugal,* "but it is difficult for those who run, to read them." Employing another characteristic tactic, Dr. Moore claims authority for his descriptions by describing himself on the title page as "A Gentleman Who Has Resided Several Years" in France, Germany, and Switzerland. But even more writers avoided the charge that they "ran" by indicating the duration of their travels in the titles of their books. Like Young's *Travels during the Years 1787, 1788, and 1789,* titles of works by Edward Wright, Frederik Hasselquist, and Philip Thicknesse frequently induced readers to trust those descriptions proclaimed to have been collected over relatively long periods of time.

Most travel writers, however, manipulated their narratives in order to avoid the appearance of having journeyed too quickly. If they proceeded slowly and attentively, they usually congratulated themselves on their deliberation; if they traveled quickly, they hid their speed and lack of attention from readers. Though spending less than a month in Dresden, Mrs. Piozzi carefully implies in her *Observations and Reflections* that she collected information about the city diligently and deliberately. Describing the gallery of the elector of Saxony, for instance, she says she spent three hours every day looking at pictures, her "feet well defended by *perlaches,* a sort of cloth clogs." Such minute, narrative detail, including her statement that she "suffered so much for the sake of seeing this collection,"[55] is obviously calculated, among other things, to convince readers of her trustworthiness. Similarly, trivial details about dining with important people may not have greatly interested Arthur Young's readers, but these bits of autobiographical information convincingly document the care with which he collected firsthand information about the society he describes in his *Travels in France.* By traveling slowly enough to insinuate himself comfortably into such circles, Young makes his travel account seem much more valuable than many of those that had previously been published. In contrast, Ann Radcliffe attempts to disguise the speed of her travels by generally glossing over her own experiences and by omitting most dates from her *Journey.* Giuseppe Baretti, one of the few eighteenth-century writers who admits that he traveled so quickly that he was unable to see certain sights, easily raised the ire of John Hawkesworth in the *Monthly Review:*

From Badajoz the Author proceeded to *Talaverola,* and from *Talaverola* to *Merida.* He says that *Merida* was once the metropolis of *Lusitanea,* and called *Augusta Emerita:* that it was in ancient times a flourishing colony of the Romans, and that many antiquities are to be seen there: none of these antiquities however did he see, and though his host told him the bridge was Roman, he had not *time* to verify his assertion. When a man travels professedly to see, and relate what he sees, it is strange to hear him say that he went through places where remarkable things were to be seen, without seeing them *for want of time.*

Travelers of Baretti's ilk inspired similar sarcasm from Samuel Pratt, who suggested that *Festina Lente* should be the motto painted on the carriage of every gentleman embarking on a lengthy journey.[56]

But even the truthful and painstaking traveler might suffer attacks on his credibility if he waited until he was safely at home before beginning his travel account. Comfortably situated in his study, he could easily add to or alter descriptions in the course of supplementing a faulty memory. Perhaps some of the confusion about autobiographical details in Addison's *Remarks* results from his waiting several years before producing a polished version of his travels. At the very least, this delay caused confusion in his recollected chronology. Toward the beginning of his book, for example, Addison describes the Italian custom of displaying in churches waxen limbs that represent the parts of the body miraculously healed through divine intercession. But he injudiciously says that he had seen such limbs in collections of antiquities throughout Italy (p. 50), thus speaking as if he had already traveled throughout the country even though, as yet, he had journeyed only as far as Padua. Similarly, in describing the comedies he saw in Venice, one of the first cities visited, he mentions a version of *El Cid* he attended in Bologna, one of the last cities on his itinerary (p. 61). In these instances Addison comes face to face with a conflict between narrative and descriptive information that every traveler who does not write "on the spot" must handle. Dr. Thomas Smith was quick to point out that the Rambler's descriptions sometimes spoil "the series of his narrations."[57] Addison seems to have recognized as much when, before quoting a classical catalog of Italian rivers, he lapses into a digression in order to explain that Silius Italicus "avoided a fault (if it be really such) which *Macrobius* has objected to *Virgil,* of passing from one place to another, without regarding their regular and natural situation, in which *Homer*'s catalogues are observed to be much more methodical and exact than *Virgil's*" (p. 88). Addison here casually refers to that passage in *The Saturnalia* (V, xv, 3-4) in which Macrobius distinguishes between the descriptive techniques of Homer and Virgil. Homer "does not jump from one place to another and so leave gaps between adjoining regions, but by proceeding thus *as though on his travels* he returns at last to his point of departure and thus completes the tale on all the lands that his muster roll embraces." By contrast, Virgil "keeps to no regular order in recounting the various districts but passes at a bound from one place to another and so disrupts the sequence of his description."[58] Homer organizes his descriptions of various regions as if he were a systematic traveler, while Virgil apparently sees no virtue in such a strict principle of organization.

Few travel writers have the honesty to confess with Coriat Junior that they returned home with notes "scarcely sufficient to wrap up a pennyworth of prunes." More common is the claim of Andrew Burnaby that his *Travels through the Middle Settlements in North America* consists of memorandums carefully composed "upon the several spots to which they refer." But if such an assertion is not truthful, it may well leave the traveler open to severe censure by readers who already know something about the present state of the country he describes. Thus the *Monthly Review*'s main complaint concerning Burnaby's *Travels* is that many of his descriptions, contrary to his opening claim, are suited "not to the situation of things in the years in which his travels were performed, but to those of earlier periods." Burnaby's treatment of the Boston Mint, for example, could not have been written on the spot, since no mint had existed in any part of British America for almost a hundred years.[59]

By stressing, sometimes honestly and sometimes not, that their books were composed "at the time and on the spots to which they relate,"[60] eighteenth-century travelers attempted to satisfy the dictum that objects described in travel accounts should be "treated of" at the time they occurred to the notice of the writer.[61] As Count Berchtold says in his *Essay to Direct and Extend the Inquiries of Patriotic Travellers* (1789), every traveler ought to insure the accuracy of his descriptions by committing them to paper "upon the spot, if the time, the place, and the circumstances will admit of it."[62] In order to follow this rule, or at least to seem to follow it, many an eighteenth-century traveler cast his narrative in the form of personal letters or journals, giving his descriptions the appearance of being immediate and hence accurate. While Defoe's *Tour thro' the Whole Island of Great Britain* and Smollett's *Travels through France and Italy* both assume an epistolary form, Defoe's *Tour* remains impersonal throughout. Though he begins each of his thirteen letters with a salutation such as "Sir—" and ends each with a complementary closing like "Sir, Your Most Humble, and Obedient Servant," the reader of his travels learns relatively little about the author and absolutely nothing about the correspondent to whom the letters supposedly are addressed. And at times Defoe even abandons his pretense of writing to a particular correspondent.[63] By contrast, Smollett reveals factual and intimate information about himself: he treats the "recipients" of his letters as personal friends, sometimes alluding to the letters they have sent him and occasionally referring to the circumstances that surround the writing of his own letters. As "proof" that they were composed on the spot, Smollett superscribes each of his letters with a date and a particular location. In another variation, Johnson's *Journey to the Western Islands of Scotland* takes the form of a personal journal, giving his narrative the appearance of an immediate and spontaneous account. In his *Journey,* Johnson in fact attacks travelers who do not at least compose notes on the spot:

> There is yet another cause of errour not always easily surmounted, though more dangerous to the veracity of itinerary narratives. . . . An observer deeply impressed by any remarkable spectacle, does not suppose, that the traces will soon vanish from his mind, and having commonly no great convenience for writing, defers the description to a time of more leisure, and better accommodation.
>
> He who has not made the experiment, or who is not accustomed to require rigorous accuracy from himself, will scarcely believe how much a few hours take from certainty of knowledge, and distinctness of imagery; how the succession of objects will be broken, how separate parts will be confused, and how many particular features and discriminations will be compressed and conglobated into one gross and general idea.

To this dilatory notation must be imputed the false relations of travellers, where there is no imaginable motive to deceive. They trusted to memory, what cannot be trusted safely but to the eye, and told by guess what a few hours before they had known with certainty.

To support this generalization, Johnson cites the example of George Wheler and Jacob Spon, who "described with irreconcilable contrariety" in their travel accounts things they surveyed together.[64] Not one to trust his memory, Johnson followed his own advice, basing his *Journey* on lengthy letters addressed to Mrs. Thrale and on a "book of remarks" written while traveling through Scotland.[65]

Ultimately, the narrative portions of eighteenth-century travel accounts, especially during the latter half of the century, subtly enabled authors to characterize themselves in such a manner as to make their books believable without necessarily causing themselves to seem too egotistical. Here the traveler can employ a specific type, casting himself usually in the role of a "philosophic traveller," a "splenetic traveller," a "sentimental traveller," or a "picturesque traveller."[66] These labels, of course, are not always mutually exclusive, the splenetic and picturesque traveler usually serving as specific subclasses of philosophic and sentimental travelers respectively. Thus philosophic and splenetic travelers share perceptive minds, while the sentimental and picturesque ones display highly refined sensibilities.

The most common stance assumed by the eighteenth-century traveler is that of the philosopher, collecting and commenting upon such information as will be of use to readers back home. Glorified by the Royal Society, this philosophical spirit in fact governed the major travel accounts of the entire century. "In the travels of a Philosopher," according to the *Monthly Review,* we find "the discoveries of science, the improvements of art, the extension of knowledge, —in a word, the general advantage of mankind, or the particular benefit of his own country, are the objects of his attention."[67] We should not, as a consequence, be surprised at seeing the "literary" Addison undertaking scientific experiments any more than we are at observing the "scientific" Arthur Young continually investigating agronomy. We likewise scarcely should be perplexed by Smollett's painstaking collection of thermometer readings at the end of his

*Travels through France and Italy.*[68] As philosophic travelers, these men seek a reputation for the "most accurate observation, and unquestionable veracity."[69] Like Dr. Johnson, they picture themselves "exercising . . . reason, testing authorities, trying conjectures, correcting inferences, and seeking out the causes of error."[70] As we might expect, Boswell found the stance of the philosophical traveler especially congenial, so much so that in meeting with General Paoli, he characterizes himself as a man whose "whole attention" is "employed in listening" and in collecting information. Such autobiographical glimpses of the philosophical traveler show him "well furnished with knowledge, and skillfully trained in the exercise of the powers of discrimination."[71] Small wonder that a Continental traveler in search of a prospective companion should advertise in the following fashion:

ADVERTISEMENT.

Iter Philosophicum. Si quis sit, in hâc natione philosphica, volens suscipere iter philosophicum per Europam, ad sapientiam acquirendam,

——mores hominum multorum cernere & urbes, inveniet comitem, natum annos 27, artium magistrum in academiâ Oxoniensi, loquentem linguas Latinam, Gallicam, & partim Italicam; intelligentem linguas Graecam & Hebraicam : pari desiderio incitatum. Epistola dirigatur (postâ solutâ) ad T. W. apud venditoreum hujus Chronici.

N. B. Haec Advertitio Latinè scribitur, ne ab illiteratis intelligatur. Odi prosanum vulgus & arceo.


And even farther from home, the philosophical spirit might easily inspire a naturalist like Michel Adanson to step beyond the usual scope of his interests in order to investigate "the natural consequence of laziness" in Senegal. Thus the philosophic traveler looks upon his own country, according to Count Berchtold, "as a sick friend, for whose relief he asks advice of all the world." And in a similar vein, Voltaire admonishes travelers to "be busied chiefly in giving faithful Accounts of all the useful Things and of the extraordinary Persons, whom to know, and to imitate, would be a Benefit to our Countrymen." Such a traveler, writing in this philosophical spirit, is a "Merchant of a noble Kind, who imports into his native Country the Arts and Virtues of other Nations."[72]

The splenetic traveler appears frequently enough in travel ac-

counts of the later eighteenth century to suggest that he is more than
simply a reflection of the writer's own personality. "There has been,
of late," said Johnson in 1778, "a strange turn in travellers to be displeased." In the view of at least some readers, Johnson borrowed
from this convention by including "nothing but complaints" in his
own *Journey*.[73] Men like Fielding, Smollett, Sharp, and their imitators employed this conventional persona so frequently that the *Analytical Review* complained in 1790 that "every inch of the continent
has been described with scrupulous exactness" by "*vapourish* travellers."[74] To be certain, travel often served as a cure for melancholy,
and many travelers were afflicted with serious medical problems
when they set out for foreign parts. Fielding, Smollett, and Sharp all
suffered from ill health, and, at the insistence of the medical profes-
sion, escaped England's winter for the warmer climes of southern
Europe. But while personal concerns are not the proper subjects of
travel accounts, the revelation of a melancholic temperament serves
a clear literary function: it makes the traveler seem the kind of person whose descriptions should be trusted. Melancholia, the "English
Malady," typically victimized only Englishmen of the upper classes.
But more important, the spleen served as a sign of acute mental
ability. "The most inquiring and contemplative" humans, according to John Hill, "suffer oftenest by this disease." The people most
subjected to it are "the grave and studious, those of a sedate temper
and enlarged understanding, the learned and wise, the virtuous and
valiant."[75] Small wonder, then, that Fielding begins his *Journal of a
Voyage to Lisbon* by describing "the most melancholy sun" he had
ever beheld and ends it in Lisbon with his splenetic ride through
"the nastiest city in the world." This is the kind of man whose observations and reflections must be trusted because of his ruling humor.
And when France and Italy raise the ire of Smollett and Sharp, their
misanthropic descriptions of foreign manners and customs show
them to be travelers who are impervious to the seductive allure of
outward appearances.

Sentimental counterparts of these melancholic travelers soon
began to see foreign countries with totally different eyes. In ridiculing such "Splenetic Travellers" as Smollett and Sharp, Sterne's *Sentimental Journey* set the stage for a number of imitators, his vain

and sentimental Yorick finding nonfictional "fellow-travellers" in Lord Gardenstone and Giuseppe Baretti. Professedly written as a gentle corrective to Smollett's *Travels*, Gardenstone's *Travelling Memorandums* (1791) describes Europe in an almost totally favorable light. "I observe," says Gardenstone, "that my old friend Smollett when overcharged at the inns, was in a violent passion and threatened vengeance by force or law, ever without redress." Gardenstone, however, finds few instances of overcharging, dealing as he does with gouging landladies in a more successful manner: "I am no unexperienced traveller," he would tell them; "I know your demand is extravagant, near double the highest usual rate: — Yet, if you insist, I shall pay you; — but be sure I shall hereafter avoid your house, — and report your behaviour to other travellers."[76] Less obviously imitative of Sterne's *Sentimental Journey*, Baretti's *Account of Manners and Customs in Italy* (1768) tries to correct the splenetic excesses most especially found in Samuel Sharp's *Letters from Italy*. Do not accept the word of travelers who "tell you, that bread and wine are bad throughout Italy," Baretti counsels readers, any more than you "credit your travel-mongers about the character of the Italians." Just as there is scarcely one melancholic traveler who does not have "a story to tell of a fellow in a church, who has stabbed divers persons,"[77] so there is hardly a sentimental traveler without a string of anecdotes about virtuous and entertaining people he encountered during the course of his travels.

The picturesque traveler, unlike his sentimental counterpart, repeatedly reveals a cultivated taste for the beauties of nature and art. His "continual display of extatic feelings"[78] shows him possessing a refined sensibility not unlike that of Ann Radcliffe's heroines. The object of his travels, as William Gilpin explains, "is beauty of every kind, which either art, or nature can produce." Basically, however, the picturesque traveler examines the scenery of nature using "the rules of painting." He looks for beauty "among all the ingredients of landscape — trees — rocks — broken-grounds — woods — rivers — lakes — plains — vallies — mountains — and distances. Ultimately, the more refined his taste grows from the *study of nature*, the more insipid are the *works of art*" to his cultivated eye.[79] Thus mooring his bark in a creek on Devannoc, Gilpin spends a full half-hour scaling the summit, where he romantically pictures himself seated "upon a rock cushioned with moss, and heath." From this vantage point, he achieves "a most amusing view" which he thereupon describes in detail. Gilpin moreover shows the effects of such sights on him when he concludes that even the Thames "falls short, in a picturesque light, of a Scotch river, with all it's rough accompaniments, pouring over rocks, and forming a thousand little foaming eddies." And when Samuel Ireland suffers "the storms and tempests of near a week" in order to return to England, he characterizes himself as a man willing to endure hardship for the sake of indulging his sensibilities.[80] These splenetic, sentimental, and picturesque travelers scarcely measure up, however, to their fictional counterparts. Though undoubtedly influenced by the misanthropic stance of Goldsmith's Mr. Drybone, the sentimental effusions of Steele's Bevil Junior, and the picturesque affectations of Radcliffe's Emily de St. Aubert, they remain but lifeless silhouettes, ruled as they are by only one dominant passion. In his *Travels,* for example, "Smollett" seems only a distant reflection of Bramble in *Humphry Clinker,* and Lord Gardenstone's *Memorandums* mimics Sterne's *Sentimental Journey* even more colorlessly.

The autobiographical information in eighteenth-century travel accounts thus serves four main functions: it provides a principle of order, conveys entertainment, proves the author is accurate and truthful, and shows him to be the sort of man whose descriptions can be trusted. Throughout most of the century, the narrative portions of travel accounts aim at a kind of equilibrium. Too little autobiographical information would cause the writer to be suspected as a "fireside," "whirlwind," or "forgetful" traveler; too much would make him seem either an egotist or a writer of fiction. In reaching for this golden mean, the traveler guards against the sins of his predecessors and contemporaries, endeavoring to prove, on the basis of internal evidence, that by blending pleasure with instruction he has not imposed upon the credibility of his readers.

To be certain, travelers and critics were not always uniform in their assessment of the proper amount of narrative information to be included in travel accounts. Addison's austere anonymity causes him to describe a brush with death in a fierce storm at sea without injecting any note of personal fear or discomfort (p. 21). Here Addison seems to mention this experience merely to describe the gulf off St. Remo, to characterize a man he encountered, and to introduce yet another classical allusion into his account. But famous men might sometimes include much more autobiographical information in their accounts without inspiring the censure of reviewers. After all, the doings of Fielding, Smollett, and Johnson understandably interested the reading public, who, in buying travel accounts, hoped to learn not only about geographical places but also about the celebrated authors themselves. The same might be said of famous members of the aristocracy—like Lord Baltimore—who, because of their reputations, would be expected to tell the truth about themselves and what they saw. In contrast, relatively unknown travelers like John Bell and Henry Ellis throughout most of the century had to remain largely silent about their own experiences lest they incite the censure of readers who would find them presumptuously egotistical.

All of these criteria, however, began to change during the last three decades of the century. Writing in 1779, Vicesimus Knox offered a dissenting view concerning the proper amount of autobiographical material in travel literature. Probably influenced by Sterne's *Sentimental Journey* more than anything else, Knox takes exception with those readers who censure travelers "for enumerating what are called trifling occurrences." Trivial experiences, according to Knox, "suggest hints; and hints, to a fertile mind, are more acceptable than formal discourses . . . because they lead the mind to exert its own activity." For this reason, Knox is pleased when a traveler "speaks in the first person, and conducts us from inn to inn, and town to town, with all the familiarity of an old acquaintance," since "every thing which concerns him interests us." The traveler brings his reader into the narrative, making him "feel as he did in all his inconveniences and distresses" and enabling him to "derive, from the whole account of small particulars, as well as great, a very valuable share and species of experience." This sentiment helps explain the request of a traveler like John Ferrar, who asks readers in 1796 to remember that "trifles light as air" serve an important role in his *Tour from Dublin to London.*[81]

By 1793 it was possible for William Roberts to try to draw a fun-

damental distinction between two kinds of travel accounts: "While
the dignity of Travel promises something like a regular course of historical inquiry, the Tour pretends only to a sprightly detail of anecdotes and memoirs." As a consequence,

> we exact from the writer of Travels a sober display of important facts, and
> a perfect development of national character and manners; but we are con-
> tent, in the livelier conduct of the Tour, with detached observations, bro-
> ken incidents, and occasional hints. We expect from the one a structure
> complete in every part; we require from the other the materials for erecting
> one, with a few scattered directions for their use and management. But we
> are by no means satisfied if the quantity only of these materials be suffi-
> cient for our present purpose; their quality must also be excellent; they
> must be well chosen, easy of application, substantial, solid, and consistent.

Though a less serious kind of composition, the Tour must display
some kind of unity, enabling the reader "to arrive at some general
judgment." According to Roberts,

> much impertinence and absurdity do frequently grow out of this indul-
> gence extended to the writers of Tours. Standing in the same relation to
> the author of Travels, as the publisher of Memoirs to the Historian, like
> them they often assume the graver carriage of their superiors; and enlarge,
> with unbecoming prolixity, on circumstances which have possession of
> their fancies and affections.

Roberts unfortunately bases his elaborate separation of "travels"
and "tours" upon a shaky generalization: in the titles of travel books,
as we have seen, the use of one of these terms scarcely insures
whether the book will be dignified or lively. Yet Roberts's discussion
accurately captures the growing shift in the direction of what would
once have been considered excessively egotistical autobiography.
We need not accept the strict distinctions themselves to perceive the
dramatic change taking place in the narrative content of travel
accounts.[82]
    This change, of course, did not occur overnight. The introduc-
tion of character types and the exhausting of novel, descriptive information undoubtedly influenced a shift in emphasis which saw
personal names of private citizens appear ever more frequently in

travel accounts toward the end of the century. While Defoe mentions only famous people in his *Tour* and Smollett relies on such circumlocutions as "Mr. A——" and "the Marquis de M——i," Gardenstone speaks at length about his friend Dr. Garden, and Anna Maria Falconbridge seems a veritable name-dropper in her *Two Voyages to Sierra Leone* (1794). And though Addison hides the name of his traveling companion, and Dr. Moore vaguely disguises the title of the duke of Hamilton, who accompanied him through Italy, Alexander Kinglake paints a lengthy and entertaining picture of Methley, his fellow traveler in Turkey. By the time Robert Southey published his *Letters Written during a Short Residence in Spain and Portugal* in 1797, significant amounts of autobiographical material had become integral parts of many travel accounts, making them seem increasingly like memoirs.

One of the most significant influences on this change must have been Sterne's *Sentimental Journey*. The number of imitations it inspired during the seventies, eighties, and nineties reflects the century's clear preference for this work over *Tristram Shandy*. While some of his imitators continued in the genre of fictional travel accounts, others with equal fervor appropriated many of his techniques for their authentic travel descriptions. Thus we find Sterne's characteristic dashes, broken statements, interruptions of sentiment, and general focusing on trivialities in fictional imitations like James Douglas's *Travelling Anecdotes* (1782) as well as in factual imitations like Lord Gardenstone's *Travelling Memorandums*. Sterne's influence was so pervasive that William Combe in 1803 could sarcastically lay down the "Rules for Tour Writing, in the True Modern Manner," by virtually describing what Sterne had achieved some thirty-five years earlier:

The tour-writer must have strong feelings. This is a sine quâ non. It does not signify what they are employed upon—whether a dead jack-ass, a monk, a nun, a grey-bearded peasant, or a lame soldier. Fine feelings can operate upon any thing, and, in all cases, the more contemptable and unaffecting the subject is, the better.[83]

"Sterne's great revelation to his age," according to J. M. S. Tompkins, was his teaching of "the significance of the small and of the fleeting."[84] Hence his imitators concentrated on subjects that Addison, Fielding, Smollett, and Johnson would have found trivial and insignificant in a travel account.

But Sterne's influence went even further. In the preface to *Sentimental Journey,* he has Yorick make his famous classification of travelers under different heads: Idle Travellers, Inquisitive Travellers, Lying Travellers, Proud Travellers, Vain Travellers, Splenetic Travellers, Travellers of Necessity, The delinquent and felonious Traveller, The unfortunate and innocent Traveller, The simple Traveller, and finally The Sentimental Traveller. But Yorick is more than merely a sentimental traveler, since — as he confesses — he breaks "in upon the confines of the *Vain* Traveller, in wishing to draw attention" toward himself. The subject of *Sentimental Journey* is largely Yorick; the reader learns much about the traveler, little about the country through which he passed. Thus Yorick is the "egotic" traveler the century had consistently condemned as being inappropriate in nonfiction travel books. This kind of egotism, however, gradually crept into the nonfiction accounts of Sterne's imitators. Samuel Paterson might hide the egotism of *Another Traveller!* by employing a pseudonym and a strange title, but this cover up largely disappeared with the republication of his travel account as *An Entertaining Journey to the Netherlands; containing a Curious and Diverting Account of the Manners and Customs of Antwerp, Alost, Breda, Brussells, Bruges, Ghent, Louvain, Utrecht, Ostend, &c. With the Forms of Travelling from Place to Place, and the Author's Adventures: The Whole Written in the Manner and Stile of the Late Mr. Laurence Sterne* (1782). And Gardenstone is ultimately able to tell readers intimate details about himself which would have disturbed even a chatty writer like Smollett.

Though the more traditional eighteenth-century voyages and travels remained long into the nineteenth century, the Victorians recognized that the literary tide had obviously turned. As a contributor to *Fraser's Magazine* noted, "in no department of our literature has a more remarkable change taken place than in what may be called the travelling department." "Instead of deriving information from a book of travels," the reader often finds that he can actually instruct the traveler concerning the country he visits. In fact, nineteenth-century travelers frequently found themselves "obliged to fall back upon their personal adventures, making their own little circle of experiences the burden of their book." "We take up a volume of modern travels," complained an anonymous author in 1843, "not expecting to discover any new views in the state of politics, religion, literature, or the fine arts." All we get is "the *res gestae* of the book writer with custom-house officers, commissionaires, and passport-people; their bill of fare at the hotel, and their score at parting; some few, and generally speaking, not very profound observations on national character; the ordinary proportion of *rechauffée* anecdote; a story—now grave, now humorous—told by the postillion; a small sprinkling of well-known names; an odd chapter of scenery and impressions, *et voila!* your book of travels."[85]

By assuming such an outline, the nineteenth-century travel account, unlike its eighteenth-century ancestor, returns to those "legends of lying travellers" which Martinus Scriblerus disliked so much. It may entertain more than its immediate forerunners, as Robert Brown wrote in 1883, but it is ultimately "too entertaining." Thus nineteenth-century travelers "are more eager to relate little adventures than to instruct the purchasers of their books."[86] The reader who wants information, after all, needs only look in a Murray or Baedeker. While the eighteenth-century cautiously guarded against the slightest bit of fictional narrative in Moore's *View of Society*, the nineteenth eagerly choose Mme. de Staël's novelistic *Corinne* (1807) as a suitable companion when traveling through Italy.[87] Hythloday, the teller of idle tales, thus returns after a long absence, causing travel literature no longer to serve as "an agreeable medium" between "mere amusement" and "abstract" learning.[88]

# III

## DESCRIPTIVE CONVENTIONS IN EIGHTEENTH-CENTURY NONFICTION TRAVEL LITERATURE

Fill thy judging ear
With bold description and with manly thought!
—Thomson, *Winter* (1730), 28-29

In the title of her *Observations and Reflections Made in the Course of a Journey through France, Italy, and Germany,* Mrs. Piozzi distinguishes between the two descriptive techniques employed in most eighteenth-century travel books. By *observations* she means specific descriptions of what she saw during her travels; by *reflections,* the philosophical, aesthetic, moral, or political thoughts these sights occasioned. Each technique aims at conveying a particular kind of instruction: observations teach facts; reflections, the significance that should be derived from the facts. After observing the perennial gaiety of Venice, Mrs. Piozzi thus reflects on how the citizens of Venice differ from those of "happy England! whence ignorance is banished by the diffusion of literature, and narrowness of notions is ridiculed even in the lowest class of life." She usually spends far more space on her reflections than on her observations, in one instance using a 75-word observation of gambling in Milan to launch into a 550-word comment that "every nation complains of the wickedness of its own inhabitants. . . till they have seen others no better." But in each instance, her reflection rests firmly on a specific observation of France, Italy, or Germany. Following this same practice, Addison describes particular religious practices in Italy which in turn lead him into general reflections on the errors of the Roman Church.

Fielding, after observing Devonshire fishermen whose catches were "so fresh, so good in kind, and so very cheap," reflects at considerable length on the relation between the consumption of fish and the operations of the British economy: "Of all the animal foods with which man is furnished, there are none so plenty as fish. . . . What then so properly the food of the poor? . . . How comes it then, to look no farther abroad for instances, that in our city of London the case is so far otherwise, that except that of sprats, there is not one poor palate in a hundred that knows the taste of fish." Though reflections, as one might expect, frequently appear in the accounts of philosophical, splenetic, and sentimental travelers, they also occur with some regularity in those written by picturesque tourists. Hence Gilpin moves from a description of deserted regions in Scotland into a lengthy consideration of such matters as population, commerce, and wealth.[1]

In their use of these two descriptive techniques, travel accounts mirror numerous philosophical and descriptive poems of the century. After observing "various scenes of life and death" in "Night I" of *Night Thoughts* (1742), for example, Edward Young reflects in detail on "the noblest truths" that each scene inspires.[2] Goldsmith similarly displays this balancing of observations with reflections in *The Traveller* (1765) and *The Deserted Village* (1770). So does Thomson in *The Seasons* (1726-1730) 1744), where after a lengthy description of the snows of winter he interjects "reflections on the wants and miseries of human life," concluding his entire work with "moral reflections on a future state."[3] As a "reflective descriptive poem," *The Seasons,* like many travel accounts, draws its "didactic" reflections from "pastoral" observations.[4]

The ratio between observations and reflections varies greatly from one travel account to another. Johann Georg Keyssler's *Travels through Germany, Bohemia, Hungary, Switzerland, Italy, and Lorraine* (German 1740; English 1756-1757), which strives to omit "nothing worthy of observation," devotes space to relatively few remarks. In contrast, Jonas Hanway's *Journal of Eight Days Journey from Portsmouth to Kingston-upon-Thames* (1765) almost entirely ignores observations, concentrating on so many "Moral and Religious" reflections that they practically "swallow up" his travels.[5]

Observations are essential in travel books; reflections, however, are not. For this reason, reviewers did not condemn Keyssler for omitting reflections, but they strenuously objected to Hanway's avoiding observations. While Keyssler, in the words of the *Critical Review,* "carries us into the most delightful countries, where the mind is constantly both entertained and instructed," presenting us "with the noblest monuments of antiquity, and all the finest and most elegant productions of later ages," Hanway handles such matters "in the slightest and most superficial manner," remaining "perpetually upon the watch for an opportunity to introduce to us his reflections." The "one quality, which no writer of travels ought to want," however, is the ability to make accurate and clear observations. Hence "a book of travels will always be found good or bad" with regard to the author's observations, not his reflections.[6]

### Observations: Descriptions of What the Traveler Saw

When Smollett advises readers to look at Keyssler's *Travels* for a description of "every thing worth seeing at Florence,"[7] he recommends what might be called an encyclopedic travel book. Keyssler attempts in his almost two thousand pages to describe every object of interest not only to the reader who sits at home, but also to the traveler who needs practical advice while on the road and in the principal cities of Europe. As its title page proclaims, his account aims at giving a "true and Just Description of the Present State" of Germany, Bohemia, Hungary, Switzerland, Italy, and Lorrain, by concentrating on "their Natural, Literary, and Political History; Manners, Laws, Commerce, Manufactures, Painting, Sculpture, Architecture, Coins, Antiquities, Curiosities of Art and Nature, &c." Filled with such a large store of useful information, Keyssler's *Travels* understandably became a handbook for tourists like Gibbon while on the Continent.[8] Revised and translated frequently during the century, its detailed indexes made it an excellent reference work, and its "Table of the Post-Stages, mentioned in the preceding Travels," even provided the eighteenth-century equivalent of a train schedule.

In trying to collect as much geographical information as possible, the eighteenth century produced many such encyclopedic accounts.

Misson's *New Voyage to Italy* (French 1691; English 1695), the "first general account of Italy,"[9] systematically describes all features of that country, while Defoe's *Tour* attempts the same task for Great Britain. Misson's *Voyage,* one of the most popular and comprehensive travel accounts of the century, explicitly contains "a Distinct Account of Whatever Appeared...Remarkable in the Places" through which its author traveled. Defoe's three-volume work—ultimately expanded into four—aims at providing "A Particular and Diverting Account of Whatever Is Curious and Worth Observation."[10] Like an almanac, it went through numerous editions, each containing updated factual information. By the time a ninth edition appeared some fifty-four years after the publication of its first volume, much of Defoe's original text had in fact disappeared. But it still remained, as the *Critical Review* indicates, "particularly distinguished by the public favour."[11]

Such encyclopedic travel accounts often have a number of common characteristics. In an attempt to describe virtually everything of interest in particular countries, they omit or abbreviate reflections, and they minimize their narratives, using them almost exclusively for the sake of ordering descriptions. So that they may make their accounts useful to readers in search of factual information about specific places, they provide detailed indexes and print itineraries, lists of posts, and the like. With an eye to the practical needs of the traveler, they generally restrict the size of their volumes to octavo or duodecimo, making them easily portable in a pocket or trunk. For the most part they remain dry repositories of vast stores of information, often collected by the traveler both from his own experiences and from the books he has read. (Such borrowing, when done, is sometimes acknowledged and sometimes not.) Only infrequently do these encyclopedias, like Defoe's *Tour,* aspire to genuine literary artistry.[12]

The diversity of information in encyclopedic travel accounts seemed staggering to Samuel Paterson, who includes the following recipe in *Another Traveller!:*

> Enter your *particulars* after the following manner;
>
> | | |
> |---|---|
> | Gates | Parish-churches |
> | Streets | Convents |

| Bridges   | Houses      |
|-----------|-------------|
| Cathedral | Inhabitants |

And your *remarkables,* as they happen to fall out. —

For example; such a picture may be seen in such a place; such a relic, in such another: — such a man was born here; and such another was buried here: — My lord such a one lives in this street; my lady such a one in that square: The Virgin Mary with her own hands, built such a chapel; and the Devil flew away with such a steeple: — The stadthouse is considerably larger than my lord mayor's mansion house; and the tower of such a church somewhat higher than St. Paul's cross.

While this may at first seem a laborious process, Paterson explains that after having visited only a few places, the traveler can save himself much trouble by remembering that one town is much the same as another. Thus he can easily imagine what various places are like, depending on little more than clichés. In Flanders, for instance, he can "suppose the cities fortified, and full of churches and convents — the churches, full of pictures; the convents, full of monks; the people, full of superstition; the streets, full of beggars." In such a fashion, a traveler like Coriat might well load his account with encyclopedic information, most having been collected rather painlessly. Moreover, he could easily steal — as did many other travel writers — from previously published books since no reader would take "the pains to detect the fraud."[13]

In a similar vein, but without irony, Count Berchtold counsels travelers to observe a wider range of subjects. The "objects deserving a traveller's attention" are so multifarious, according to Berchtold, that they must be divided into groups "according to their importance." Berchtold thus places into four successively less important classes those "objects" which (1) contribute to "the welfare of Mankind," (2) aid the "prosperity of a traveller's native country," (3) assist the traveler in achieving "personal advantages and improvements," and (4) give the traveler what Berchtold calls "ornamental knowledge" of foreign countries. In order to collect the most helpful information, the traveler should ask questions concerning a staggering number of topics including geography, population, the state of the peasantry, agriculture, cattle in general, black cattle, sheep,

Political Review, Valuation, &c. relative to AGRICULTURE.

| Names of the various Productions of the Country. | Their lowest Price. | Their highest Price. | Amount of the Annual Crop of each Production. | Value of the Annual Crop of each Production on an Average. | Annual Consumption of each Production. | Quantity annually exported of each Production. | Country where each Production is carried to, and in what Quantity and Value on an Average. | Name of the Province where each Production is cultivated. | Number of Acres employed for the Cultivation of each Production. | Price of an Acre of Ground proper for the Culture of each Production. | Rent of an Acre of Ground proper for the Culture of each Production. | Degree of Fertility, viz. how many Bushels for one Bushel of Seed. |
|---|---|---|---|---|---|---|---|---|---|---|---|---|
|  |  |  |  |  |  |  |  |  |  |  |  |  |

Figure 3. Table facing p. 139 of Volume I in Count Leopold Berchtold's *Essay to Direct and Extend the Inquiries of Patriotic Travellers* (London, 1789).

woods, mines, manufactures, inland and foreign trade, and other such matters.[14] Concerning each of these subjects, Berchtold also suggests specific questions which should be asked. Under "agriculture," for example, he lists 206 detailed queries, and he provides a convenient table (see fig. 3) which the traveler ought to complete by providing appropriate data.

The favorable reception enjoyed by Berchtold's *Essay* indicates that his suggestions, outrageously complex as they may seem, were taken seriously by his contemporaries.[15] Berchtold, after all, simply collects the kinds of advice that had been directed at travelers in general and English travelers in particular for almost two centuries. William Davison's "Most Notable and Excellent Instrvctions for Traueillers" probably served as his earliest model. Used to introduce *Profitable Instructions; Describing What Speciall Obseruations Are To Be Taken by Trauellers in All Nations* (1633), Davison's essay merely catalogs the kinds of information which should be gleaned by travelers. After dividing all enquiries into three groups—"The Countrey," "The People," "The policy and gouernment"—Davison explains that in examining the country, for example, the traveler should consider:

I.   The scituation          1  Island, or continent;
     & nature thereof;           neere, or far frō the sea.
     As whether it be        2  Plaine, or hilly; full or
                                 scarce of Riuers.

II   Quantity,      1 length,
                    2 bredth,              where
                    3 circuit,

                                        1 Forme.
                           also the
                                        2 climat.

III. How it confineth with other Countries; and,
         1 What these Countrie are.
         2 What their strength and riches are.
         3 Wherein they consist.
         4 Whether friends or enemies.

IIII.   The fertility thereof, and what commodities it doth either,

 1 Yeeld and bring forth, and what part thereof hath bin
 
                or is $\begin{cases} 1. & \text{Consumed at home.} \\ \\ 2. & \text{Vented abroad} \end{cases}$

 2 Want; and how, and from whence it is supplyed.
 
           1.   Nature.

V.      Of what strength it is, and how defended against the attempts of
        bordering neighbors, either by

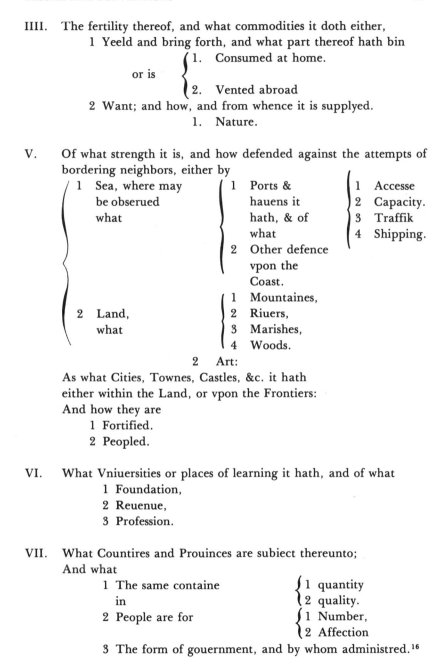

| 1 | Sea, where may be obserued what | 1 | Ports & hauens it hath, & of what | 1 | Accesse |
|   |   | | | 2 | Capacity. |
|   |   | | | 3 | Traffik |
|   |   | 2 | Other defence vpon the Coast. | 4 | Shipping. |
| 2 | Land, what | 1 | Mountaines, | | |
|   |   | 2 | Riuers, | | |
|   |   | 3 | Marishes, | | |
|   |   | 4 | Woods. | | |

          2   Art:

As what Cities, Townes, Castles, &c. it hath
either within the Land, or vpon the Frontiers:
And how they are
 1 Fortified.
 2 Peopled.

VI.     What Vniuersities or places of learning it hath, and of what
          1 Foundation,
          2 Reuenue,
          3 Profession.

VII.    What Countires and Prouinces are subiect thereunto;
        And what

 1 The same containe in $\begin{cases} 1 & \text{quantity} \\ 2 & \text{quality.} \end{cases}$

 2 People are for $\begin{cases} 1 & \text{Number,} \\ 2 & \text{Affection} \end{cases}$

 3 The form of gouernment, and by whom administred.[16]

Though similar instructions appear in the Royal Society's "Directions for Sea-men, Bound for Far Voyages" (1666) and in Robert
Boyle's *General Heads for the Natural History of a Country . . . for
the Use of Travellers and Navigators* (1692), undoubtedly the greatest influence on Berchtold's *Essay* was Bishop Tucker's *Instructions
for Travellers* (1757). Berchtold frequently quotes Tucker, and he
probably borrowed directly from Tucker his format, which consists
of lists of questions the inquisitive traveler should answer. While
more modest in scope than Berchtold's two-volume work, Tucker's
pamphlet clearly points to similar objectives for the "patriotic" traveler: "he should constantly bear in mind the grand Maxim, That the
Face of every Country through which he passes, the Looks, Numbers, and Behaviour of the People, their general Clothing, Food,
and Dwelling, their Attainments in Agriculture, Manufactures, Arts
and Sciences, are the Effects and Consequences of some certain
Causes." The traveler must, as a consequence, "investigate and discover" these causes, considering "whether, and how far the said
Effects may be ascribed to the natural Soil and Situation of the
Country. — To the peculiar Genius and singular Inventions of the
Inhabitants. — To the Public Spirit and Tenor of their Constitution,
— or to the Religious Principles established, or tolerated among
them." Tucker, himself an expert economist, concludes his pamphlet with instructions specifically geared to helping the traveler discover "the comparative Poverty, or Riches" of any "City, Town, or
Country":

1. Let the Traveller enquire the relative Price both of Land, and
Money....
2. Let the Traveller observe the Condition of the public Inns on the
great Roads....
3. Let the Traveller make the like Observations and Inquiries concerning the Number of Waggons, which pass and re-pass the Road....
4. Let him be particularly attentive to the Quantity and Quality of the
Wares to be found in the Shops of the Country Towns, and Villages....
5. Let the Traveller also enquire into the State of Living in Cities and
Towns....
6. Let him further observe both in Town and Country, Whether the
Generality of the Inhabitants decorate, or keep neat the Outside of their

Houses; and bestow some Kind of Ornament on their Grounds and Gardens....

7. Lastly, let him particularly inquire, Whether Tenants in the Country usually pay their Rents in Money, or in Produce....[17]

Such encyclopedic information, if carefully collected and verified, contributes to the well-being of the traveler's native country by propagating useful knowledge concerning foreign lands.

But in attempting to make his book as comprehensive as possible, the encyclopedic traveler often violates the overriding demand for novelty in travel accounts. Keyssler's descriptions are thus so laboriously circumstantial that Smollett could never "peruse them, without suffering the headach, and recollecting the old observation, that the German genius lies more in the back than in the brain." Frequently forced to visit "only those countries which every man visits," seeing only "what every man sees," these encyclopedic travelers with some degree of regularity blatantly steal descriptions from other authors.[18] In overlooking nothing, according to Fielding, they scarcely serve as agreeable companions for a man of sense. Consequently, they are frequently avoided by the ideal travel writer of the century, who in his fear of being called "a ridiculous repeater of what thousands have said before," tries his best to satisfy the "love of novelty and variety" among readers.[19]

The demand for novelty was so strong, in fact, that it became one of the chief criteria by which eighteenth-century reviewers evaluated travel books. In discussing Smollett's *Compendium of Authentic and Entertaining Voyages,* the *Critical Review* explains that voyages and travels are universally read because they form "a Species of writing which is adapted to all capacities, which affords continual food to that curiosity which is so natural to the mind of man, and that love of novelty which is inseparable from it."[20] But while Smollett's *Compendium* passes the *Critical Review*'s test for novelty, a book like Edward Thompson's *Sailor's Letters* (1766) fails on the grounds that it lacked anything new. Similarly, Dr. Johnson's *Journey* gratifies readers with "new scenes," but Mrs. Piozzi's *Observations and Reflections* bores at least some because it contains "nothing so very different from other accounts, particularly Dr. Moore's."[21] In discussing *Observations Made in a Journey through the Western Counties of Scotland* (1793), still another reviewer sums up this demand for novelty by advising Robert Heron to consider "for the benefit of any future publication, that it is not every opinion which may be formed in his mind, or every object he may cast his eyes upon, which is worthy of being presented to the public, but only what is new, striking, and relevant to his subject."[22] The traveler needed novel descriptions to make his account not only instructive but also pleasant. "Every thing that is new or uncommon raises a Pleasure in the Imagination," says Addison in *Spectator* 412, "because it fills the Soul with an agreeable Surprise, gratifies its Curiosity, and gives it an Idea of which it was not before possest."

The quest for novelty, combined with the popularity of the genre, inevitably created a difficult problem for many aspiring travel writers. As the *Critical Review* explains,

When an ingenious and enterprizing traveller has visited an unknown climate, and, at his return, amused his countrymen with a minute description of its natural productions, its artificial curiosities, and the habits, customs, and manners, of the natives, he naturally excites attention. But when another pursues the same road, and describes the same objects, his narrative is received with much more indifference. . . . The first is more eagerly read than the second; though, with respect to merit, the latter may not be inferior to the former. Curiosity is gratified by the first publication, and the charm of novelty, the charm which stimulates, delights, and actuates, all mankind, is dissolved.[23]

In seeing "what it is expected a man should see,"[24] English travel writers on the traditional grand tour through France and Italy — with glances at Switzerland, Germany, and The Low Countries — soon began to lament that relatively little new information could, after all, be obtained concerning these countries.[25]

In light of such problems, travel writers during the second half of the century began discovering "new" countries like Spain, Portugal, Mecklenburg, Sweden, Russia, and Corsica, thus assuring that their accounts of these faraway places would contain the novelty readers demanded. Judging "the accounts of Spain hitherto published in the English language . . . to be very imperfect," Giuseppe Baretti in 1770 sought for the first time to describe the Iberian peninsula accurately and in detail. His description of this least known European country, as Dr. Johnson termed it, earned him the *Critical Review*'s compliments on his novel subject and inspired a large number of imitations, all hoping to find somewhere along Spanish roads "such subjects as have never before been published."[26] On a similar search for novelty, Thomas Nugent gave the British public, which previously "knew no more of Mecklenburg than they did of Lapland," its first detailed picture of that tiny German state in his *Travels* (1768), and Nathaniel Wraxall when composing his *Cursory Remarks* judiciously directed his steps away from the grand tour to those regions "where the greatest novelties were to be expected."[27] Wraxall's accounts of Sweden, Russia, and the less-traveled areas of France aim at exciting among readers novelty and admiration—those two powers most conducive to pleasure—by studiously avoiding "the ground usually trodden by the English, in their passage from Calais into Italy," it being "too well known to afford . . . any information."[28] And hoping to compile the sort of novel travel account Johnson wanted to see, Boswell shrewdly appraised the British thirst for information about remote places by "discovering" Corsica for his readers. Earning him fame as "Corsica Boswell," his description remained, even a hundred years after its publication, "still by far the best account of the island."[29]

While these travelers were describing the far corners of the Continent, still others began to discover yet another novel country, but one nearer home than Spain or Corsica. Before the 1750s, surprisingly few Englishmen of wealth and social position had traveled extensively throughout their own country, and fewer still had described their homeland in accounts of their travels. As late as 1763, the *Critical Review* could lament with only a bit of overstatement that little was known about the topography of Great Britain, that the geography of Scotland was only then becoming settled, and that the inland parts of Ireland still remained as unknown as Africa.[30] Indeed, before the eighteenth century, scarcely any Englishman had seen much of the British Isles unless required to do so because of his business.[31] By the end of the century, however, tours through England, Scotland, Wales, and occasionally Ireland had become

fashionable diversions among the upper classes.[32] Like Richardson's
Mr. B——, many Englishmen discovered the pleasure and improvement to be derived from seeing their own country, and like Pamela,
some of them committed their descriptions to paper.[33]

The English traveler, always in search of novelty, looked into
remoter and more obscure corners of his country as the century progressed. Captain Edward Burt, for example, virtually discovered the
Scottish Highlands in his *Letters from a Gentleman in the North of
Scotland,* and Dr. Johnson did the same for the Hebrides, the only
previous account of them being Martin Martin's long outdated and
seriously flawed *Description of the Western Islands of Scotland*
(1703). "It is not a century," claimed the *Critical Review* in 1796,

since the inhabitants of the southern part of this island knew little else of
their northern neighbours, than that they were very poor and very dirty;
and if a scattered traveller now and then made his way amongst the rocks
and torrents of so wild a country, his complaints of the miserable accommodations he was obliged to submit to, and the little civilisation of the
country, repressed all desire to be acquainted with a people, whose habits
and manner of living the pampered Englishman, basking on the sunny side
of the hedge, considered as equally remote from his own, with those of the
inhabitants of Kamschatka or Caffraria.

But travelers like Burt, Johnson, Pennant, and Gilpin altered all
this, making "the tourist and the tourist-reader" as familiar with the
lakes of Scotland as they were with the banks of the Thames.[34]
Joseph Cradock similarly led the discovery of Wales in his *Letters
from Snowdon,* and William Hutchinson's *Excursion to the Lakes,
in Westmoreland and Cumberland* (1774) virtually advertised the
"Tour of the Lakes," causing it to become "the *ton* of the present
hour."[35] Predictably, "Home Travels" like Thomas Pennant's *Tour
in Wales* proved to Englishmen that Britain "vies with most countries in natural curiosities, as well as in the elegant and useful works
of art." By leading natives of Britain through their own land, Pennant could invalidate the reproaches "of sensible foreigners, who
complain that the English travel to every part of Europe in search of
trifling curiosities, while they neglect or overlook the wonderful
productions of nature and art at home."[36]

Most of these "discoverers," feeling the need to compile as much information as possible about novel places, published encyclopedic travel accounts. Having no fear of repeating previous travel accounts, works like Boswell's include "what would nowadays be looked for on the subject in an encyclopaedia, in manuals of history and geography, and in Murray or Baedeker."[37] Burt's *Letters from a Gentleman* likewise conveys a wide variety of information about the Highlands, including "*Facts* and *Circumstances* intirely New to the Generality of People in *England,* and little known in the Southern Parts of *Scotland.*"[38] Such works, as a consequence, achieved a wide popularity primarily because of their comprehensive treatment of totally novel information.

Since not every traveler could discover a virgin geographical region, however close to home, the reading public's insistence upon novelty sent many of them in search of something new to say about previously described areas. For instance, Addison uses the classics as his novel principle of selection. Taking care "*to consider the several passages of the ancient Poets, which have any relation to the Places and Curiosities*" encountered during his travels in Italy (p. 18), he describes Italy in a fashion employed by no other English writer. Other travelers employ similarly restrictive and novel principles of selection: Arthur Young focuses on agricultural descriptions, while Edward Wright confines himself to painting and sculpture. Likewise, Charles Burney concentrates on musical matters, Thomas Pennant on natural history, Johann Jakob Ferber on mineralogy, and Andrew Ducarel on antiquities. Still other travelers center their works on prisons and hospitals, the effects of the French Revolution, and the origin and progress of poetry in Spain.[39] By having "a particular pursuit in his head," each of these men aimed at making his account a useful repository of fresh knowledge.[40]

Fashion and the success of a previous traveler also frequently dictated the kind of descriptions that found their way into travel accounts. Topham, for example, could humorously complain in his *Letters from Edinburgh* (1776): "Some years ago every man who travelled went in the character of a Builder, taking the measure of this dome, and that temple, and then relating to his countrymen the height, circumference, &c. of each." But in the early 1770s, Topham continues, the typical traveler found himself acting "the part of a Farmer; he enquires after the crops, turns over the soil, and tastes the manure, for the benefit of his countrymen."[41] And just as many Englishmen must have ruined their taste buds in search of the success enjoyed by Arthur Young's agricultural tours, so also many undoubtedly destroyed their eyesight looking for the picturesque scenes that had made William Gilpin so famous.

During the 1760s and 1770s, travel books most commonly employed a new principle of selection, variously termed "men and manners," "manners and customs," "character and manners," or some synonymous expression. Limiting himself to this topic, the traveler primarily attempts to describe the inhabitants of foreign countries, focusing on such matters as their habits, customs, laws, and religions. Like Rasselas, his "business is with man." But like Rasselas, he must also realize that "to know any thing . . . we must know its effects; to see men we must see their works, that we may learn what reason has dictated or passion has incited, and find what are the most powerful motives of action." For this reason, travelers who define manners and customs at times find themselves measuring "fragments of temples" and tracing "choked aqueducts," but always in hopes of capturing the spirit of the people they describe.[42]

These descriptions of "manners and customs" in travel books derive from a clearly defined classical precedent dating back to Ulysses, the archetypal wanderer. As the *Critical Review* explains, the main advantage resulting from travel is the attainment of "that universal science and true wisdom" which Ulysses gained by looking "with discerning eyes upon the cities and manners of many men."[43] According to Abraham Anquetil-Duperron, only the man like Ulysses who has "Thro' various kingdoms stray'd. / Their manners, laws, and customs weigh'd," can understand national peculiarities or judge national errors and prejudices. For this reason, the Marquis of Chastellux suitably selects "Multorumque hominum vidit urbes, & mores cognavit" and its Greek equivalent as the mottos for his *Travels in North-America* (1787), and Nathaniel Wraxall carefully explains in the opening letter of his Baltic tour that the description of manners provides "the most elevated and rational pleasure."[44] Yet while some travelers, like Nugent and Johnson, explicitly sought to emulate Homer's hero, *The Odyssey* scarcely served as an adequate model for their accounts. Homer, in the overstated words of Fielding, was but a "confounder and corrupter" of travel literature by virtue of his introduction of romance into it.[45] Such a sin was unforgivable in the convention-conscious eyes of the eighteenth century.

Substituting facts for Homeric romance, descriptions of manners and customs dominated the market for several decades. Numerous works like Sharp's *Letters from Italy, Describing the Customs and Manners of That Country* contain the key terms in their titles, while others like Wraxall's *Cursory Remarks* state in opening letters that they constantly report "those events which elucidate the characters or manners" of foreign countries. All of these travel accounts, whether blatantly or not, pay at least lip service to the belief that "the great aim of man, and the most important object of travel" is the knowledge of mankind. For this reason, works of these philosophical travelers make previous ones "appear comparatively trifling" with their "jejune and uninteresting" descriptions. Even Dr. Johnson ultimately focuses his *Journey* in this fashion by investigating "the remote sources of the genius and character of the inhabitants" of Scotland. As a perceptive observer of men and manners, Johnson thus avoids the kind of "bare description" that had characterized earlier travel accounts.[46]

Despite the popularity of these accounts of manners and customs, the introduction of yet another novel topic provided the most striking of all changes in eighteenth-century travel literature. Beginning in the 1770s, travelers for the first time turned extensively, and sometimes almost exclusively, to descriptions of the beauties of nature. While Defoe and Boswell occasionally allude to rural charms, they scarcely describe them to the extent and in the manner that William Gilpin does in his books. Paying relatively little attention to buildings, picture galleries, and manners of distant and not-so-distant people, travelers now begin to roam Great Britain and the Continent in search of the sublimity and grandeur of the countryside. No longer loaded with facts, their accounts become collections of evocative descriptions focusing on the almost poetic qualities of mountains, forests, rivers, and lakes.

Critics have customarily attributed this change in travel books merely to a datable shift in the eighteenth century's aesthetic appreciations. Christopher Hussey thus defines 1768 as the landmark year in which John Dalton and John Brown sent travelers like Arthur Young and Thomas Gray to the Lakes in search of picturesque beauty. Edward Cox dates this transition two years later, with Joseph Cradock's *Letters from Snowdon* initiating "tourism for the purpose of enjoying scenery." George B. Parks suggests 1779, the year in which H.-B. de Saussure published the first volume of *Voyages dans les Alpes*. Before arriving at this date, Parks concludes that earlier travelers like Addison had "little use" for scenery except when "organized by art." Like Bernardin de Saint-Pierre's *Voyage* (1773), Augustan travel accounts characteristically lack "that rapturous response to nature which one would expect in a properly attuned traveller of the later eighteenth century." But proof that earlier travelers had little use for natural beauty rests on a simplistic reading of their accounts. We cannot surmise that Addison disliked the countryside from his regret at traveling through Tyrol, which "had very little to Entertain . . . besides the natural Face of the Country."[47] Such a statement simply bespeaks his disappointment at not being able to satisfy the generic demands of his work for readers who expected to find factual information about places like Munich, Augsburg, and Ratisbon.

By mid-century, to be sure, travelers were beginning to exhaust their readers' interest in superficial descriptions of such places. "The same cities, towns, ruins, and rivers," complained Goldsmith, appear with "disgusting repetition" in numerous travel accounts. As a corrective, he suggests that future travelers visit the identical places in order to examine "the manners and mechanic inventions, and the imperfect learning of the inhabitants." The quest for novelty thus in part begins to transform the formal expectations of readers, who now increasingly anticipate descriptions of men and manners in travel accounts. But repeated over and over, even this topic in turn comes to lose its novelty. Although "the manners and customs of foreign nations afford a more ample field" of observation than "descriptions of towns," observed the *Critical Review* in 1771, manners and customs "are not inexhaustible, and though the account of them may be interwoven with interesting incidents, we soon become sensible of that disgust, which attends the frequent repetition of the same remarks."[48] By the 1770s travel writers had therefore begun to deplete all of "the Worthiest Objects of Inquiry" in many parts of the world. What remained was simply that class of "ornamental knowledge" Berchtold advised should be pursued only "without neglecting" such important subjects as contribute to the welfare of mankind, of the traveler's native country, and of the traveler himself.[49] Whereas mountains, plains, and rivers had formerly served to instruct the reader concerning their utility as boundaries, sources of food, defenses, and their influences on national manners and customs, these natural features now become the primary topics of description, serving for the most part simply as a source of amusement for the traveler and his readers. Thus the quest for novel subject matter plays an important role in this new interest in natural beauty. Pleasure alone now begins to supplant the Horatian ideal of pleasurable instruction as the artistic goal of travel literature.

These new concentrations upon national manners and natural beauty demanded from writers new descriptive techniques and different approaches to the collection of information. Travelers had to begin experimenting with increasingly difficult kinds of descriptions and increasingly demanding methods of gathering facts. Their accounts, as a consequence, frequently become more "literary," and the travelers themselves often achieve a higher degree of sophistication in their observations.

The traveler during the latter half of the century inherited from his encyclopedic predecessors some unsatisfactory descriptive techniques. In resorting to enumerations of geographical characteristics, lists of meticulous measurements, summaries of historical significances, compilations of inscriptions, passages of poetical quotations, and the like, the encyclopedic traveler collected information without considering its effect on the mind of the reader. At best, such descriptions become a bewildering "labyrinth or rather desert" of dry facts, all too often occasioning ridicule and parody from readers.[50] Thus one critic hurls enumerative descriptions "to th' back side of the world,"[51] while another makes fun of travelers repeatedly measuring the number of feet to the top of every building.[52] Who cares, asks Samuel Paterson in the same vein, how often *"Bruges,*

*Ghent, Alost,* &c. &c. &c. &c. &c. &c. &c. &c. &c. [have] changed
their masters; been taken and retaken; conquered and ceded"? The
inclusion of such historical facts makes travel books simply "a species
of literary fraud."[53] Inscriptions likewise "cost nothing—but the
pains of transcribing; and pay well those who affect bloated learning,"[54] while quotations from the poets often transform travel
accounts into mere poetic scrapbooks.[55] All of these descriptions, as
Paterson points out in an exaggerated fashion, "may be done by
anyone." But while they help "greatly to swell and set off a book,"
they always fail to convey a clear picture of the countries being described. "The truth is," says the *Critical Review,* "a traveller may
visit a country; he may give us an account of its soil, product, mountains, rivers, climates, bearings, and the like; and yet be unable to
convey a true or satisfactory account of the places he visits." "What
man," asks Coriat Junior, "ever conveived a picture, or a statue,
such as it really is, by the best description that could be written of
it?" For this reason, Lien Chi Altangi remains totally silent in *The
Citizen of the World* concerning "buildings, roads, rivers, and
mountains." Few readers, after all, find pleasure in learning that a
fallen Egyptian column measures "exactly five feet nine inches
long."[56]

As an alternative approach, the collection of information concerning manners and customs demanded significantly more care
and talent. While previous travelers had moved rapidly and had
seemingly desired "very little more than the face" of the country,
these new travelers required "long usage and much observation" in
order to "speak with tolerable precision of the manners and customs
of a people."[57] Though many modern travelers were content to ex-
pound on such subjects as "the moral and religious notions" of a foreign country after only "three months residence," others scrupu-
lously aimed at carefully documented conclusions. The "intelligent
and sagacious" traveler, according to the *Analytical Review,* needs
almost superhuman precision and diligence when explaining national manners: he must spend "a considerable length of time" and
mix "on intimate terms, with all ranks and orders; he must know the
language accurately; he must have some previous knowledge of the
history and laws of the people with whom he wishes to be acquainted,
and must be superior to those narrow prejudices, which confine all

our ideas of truth, propriety, and excellence to *home*."[58] Not always possessing these qualities, travelers investigating men and manners frequently lapsed into silly mistakes: Edward Topham, for example, misinterprets funeral practices in Edinburgh, and Samuel Sharp becomes embroiled in a "book fight" concerning Italian manners and customs.[59] In the hands of simpleminded travelers, these descriptions frequently rest on shopworn commonplaces. "An Englishman" is customarily "serious and morose: a Scotchman proud and overbearing, an Irishman a fortunehunter: a Frenchman, a fop, with paper-ruffles and no shirt. A Spaniard, grave, stiff and haughty; a Russian, bearish; an Italian, effeminate, a fidler, &c. &c." Travelers similarly are apt to report that France is known for levity, Spain for pride, and Italy for treachery, or that

the $\left\{ \begin{array}{l} \text{Germans drink} \\ \text{French sing,} \\ \text{Spaniards sigh} \\ \text{Italians sleep} \end{array} \right\}$ away grief.[60]

Though often criticized for their failures, these travelers in search of men and manners aimed at a more sophisticated kind of account than had their more superficial predecessors. As James Beattie explains, "One can easily dig to the root of a plant, but it is not so easy to penetrate the motive of an action."[61]

While descriptions of manners and customs require great wisdom, unprejudiced objectivity, and careful observation, they scarcely demand the kind of literary skill needed to convey accurate and engaging pictures of natural settings. As Henry Skrine explains, writers encounter more difficulty recording the "scenes nature has produced" than describing "the state of society, and the manners which prevail" among remote people. In the hands of a poet like Thomson, who describes "general Nature," the limitation of language in recording natural beauty simply serves as a traditional topos:

Who can paint
Like Nature? Can imagination boast,
Amid its gay creation, hues like hers?
Or can it mix them with that matchless skill,

And lose them in each other, as appears
In every bud that blows? If fancy then
Unequal fails beneath the pleasing task,
Ah, what shall language do? ah, where find words
Tinged with so many colours and whose power,
To life approaching, may perfume my lays?

But this problem becomes more serious in the hands of a travel writer, who must describe "particular Nature," not the "general Nature" of the poet. Ann Radcliffe, for example, confesses that she has trouble describing various landscapes for her readers: "A repetition of the same images of rock, wood and water, and the same epithets of grand, vast and sublime, which necessarily occur, must appear tautologous, on paper, though their archetypes in nature, ever varying in outline, or arrangement, exhibit new visions to the eye, and produce new shades of effect on the mind." Mrs. Piozzi expresses a similar frustration concerning the limitations of words: The country near Lyons "is really beautiful; but descriptions are *so* fallacious, one half despairs of communicating one's ideas as they are: for either well-chosen words do not present themselves, or being well-chosen they detain the reader, and fix his mind on *them,* instead of the things described." In fact, the describer of natural beauty faces an entirely new problem, since he seeks to move his readers without necessarily educating them. As Nathaniel Wraxall points out, the traveler is hence frequently faced with "objects which to be felt must be seen, and before which language sinks unequal."[62]

For many eighteenth-century readers, Patrick Brydone was the first travel writer to solve this dilemma by discovering how to "paint / Like Nature" in his *Tour through Sicily and Malta.* Though occasionally resorting to some of the more traditional forms of description, Brydone usually finds them largely unsatisfactory. No sooner has he measured Mount Etna and detailed the sizes of several other landmarks, than he denies that this sort of description can possibly convey anything but a very imperfect idea of his subjects. "To mark out the precise dimensions with a mathematical exactness, where there is nothing very remarkable," he apologizes, "must surely be but a dry work, both to the writer and reader." As a consequence, he turns to a hitherto novel descriptive technique, at least in travel literature: "I shall therefore content myself (I hope it will content you too) with endeavouring to communicate, as entire as possible, the same impression I myself shall receive, without descending too much to particulars; or fatiguing myself or you with the mensuration of antique walls, merely because they are such." While this kind of description should please his readers, Brydone nevertheless confesses its inherent difficulties:

I own I despair of success: Few things I believe in writing being more difficult than thus "s'emparer de l'imagination," to seize, — to make ourselves masters of the reader's imagination, to carry it along with us through every scene, and make it in a manner congenial with our own; every prospect opening upon him with the same light, and arising in the same colours, and at the same instant too, as upon us: For where descriptions fail in this, the pleasure of reading them must be very trivial.

His apologies laid aside, Brydone then attempts a verbal sketch of Mount Etna. The result is typical of the new kind of evocative description that delighted his readers:

No imagination has dared to form an idea of so glorious and so magnificent a scene. Neither is there on the surface of this globe, any one point that unites so many awful and sublime objects. — The immense elevation from the surface of the earth, drawn as it were to a single point, without any neighbouring mountain for the senses and imagination to rest upon; and recover from their astonishment in their way down to the world. This point or pinnacle, raised on the brink of a bottomless gulph, as old as the world, often discharging rivers of fire, and throwing out burning rocks, with a noise that shakes the whole island. Add to this, the unbounded extent of the prospect, comprehending the greatest diversity and the most beautiful scenery in nature; with the rising sun, advancing in the east, to illuminate the wondrous scene.

The whole atmosphere by degrees kindled up, and shewed dimly and faintly the boundless prospect around. Both sea and land looked dark and confused, as if only emerging from their original chaos; and light and darkness seemed still undivided; till the morning by degrees advancing, completed the separation. The stars are extinguished, and the shades disappear. The forests, which but now seemed black and bottomless gulphs,

from whence no ray was reflected to shew their form or colours, appear a
new creation rising to the sight; catching life and beauty from every increasing beam. The scene still enlarges, and the horizon seems to widen
and expand itself on all sides; till the sun, like the great Creator, appears in
the east, and with his plastic ray completes the mighty scene. — All appears
enchantment.[63]

By portraying the natural setting as possessing activity and by introducing evocative terms like *glorious, magnificent, awful,* and *sublime,* Brydone causes the reader to become imaginatively involved
and to fill in, as it were, the more particular parts of the description.
Mixing past and present verb tenses, Brydone aims at leading the
reader's imagination through every scene, integrating the time during which Brydone observed the scene with the time during which
his reader experiences it.

   With this novel descriptive approach, Brydone attempts to over-
come Burke's objections to travel literature. "Suppose we were to
read," says Burke,

a passage to this effect. "The river Danube rises in a moist and mountain-
ous soil in the heart of Germany, where winding to and fro it waters several
principalities, until turning into Austria and leaving the walls of Vienna it
passes into Hungary; there with a vast flood augmented by the Saave and
the Drave it quits Christendom, and rolling through the barbarous countries which border on Tartary, it enters by many mouths into the Black
sea." In this description many things are mentioned, as mountains, rivers,
cities, the sea, &c. But let anybody examine himself, and see whether he
has had impressed on his imagination any pictures of a river, mountain,
watery soil, Germany, &c.

If these descriptions seem like architectural blueprints, aimed at
complete factual accuracy, Brydone's more often resemble rough
sketches like those of Claude Lorrain, which provide outlines, evoke
moods, but allow the observer imaginatively to fill in many particulars. Earlier descriptions loaded the mind with facts. Brydone's impress the mind with images, transcending what Lessing calls the
barrier between painting and poetry. Brydone describes "objects or
parts of objects which exist in space" by evocatively treating them in
terms of the actions they exert on the mind of the perceiver.[64]

Critical acclaim amply rewarded Brydone for his innovative descriptions. Writing in the *Monthly Review,* Ralph Griffiths became quite ecstatic as a result of Brydone's treatment of Mount Etna:

What an exquisite description has our ingenious Author given us of his ascent to the summit of this supremely glorious and dreadful mountain! We see every thing which he saw, we feel all that he felt, we share in his fatigues, and we partake of his raptures. Indeed, Mr. B. the Reviewers, their Readers, and the public in general, are highly obliged to you, for the delight you have afforded them!

As a consequence of such passages, Griffiths concluded that *A Tour through Sicily and Malta* "contains more good sense, more knowledge, more variety of entertainment, than is to be found in *most* works of the kind: — in truth, we cannot, at present, recollect *one* that can be put in competition with it."[65] By combining "the two grand qualities necessary to a good traveller — curiosity to see, and ingenuity to describe," Brydone earned the praise of readers like Dr. Johnson and Fanny Burney, making his *Tour* one of the most popular and influential of all books published during the second half of the century.[66] By 1850 it had appeared in at least twenty-three English editions, had been translated into French, German, and Dutch, and had found its way into a number of important collections.

Following Brydone's lead, subsequent travelers devoted increasingly greater amounts of space to such imaginative descriptions. In her lone travel book, for example, Mrs. Radcliffe cultivated many of the same techniques that she employed in her novels, techniques that made her works famous not for "a story, nor a character, nor a moral truth, but a mood" generated by descriptions.[67] Her *Journey Made in the Summer of 1794* borrows, in the words of the *Critical Review,* "partly of painting" in order to impart "the enthusiasm of the author . . . to the reader." Passages like the following earn the special praise of reviewers:

The calm continued during the day, and the sun set with uncommon grandeur among clouds of purple, red and gold, that, mingling with the serene azure of the upper sky, composed a richness and harmony of colouring which we never saw surpassed. It was most interesting to watch the progress of evening and its effect on the waters; streaks of light scattered among the dark western clouds, after the sun had set, and gleaming in long reflection on the sea, while a grey obscurity was drawing over the east, as the vapours rose gradually from the ocean. The air was breathless; the tall sails of the vessel were without motion, and her course upon the deep scarcely perceptible; while, above, the planet Jupiter burned with steady dignity, and threw a tremulous line of light on the sea, whose surface flowed in smooth waveless expanse. Then, other planets appeared, and countless stars spangled the dark waters. Twilight now pervaded air and ocean, but the west was still luminous, where one solemn gleam of dusky red edged the horizon, from under heavy vapours.[68]

Though such a verbal picture is unlike any in Addison's travel account, Mrs. Radcliffe's descriptive technique bears a striking similarity to that found in the "poetic" parts of *Remarks on Italy*. Mrs. Radcliffe merely invents for herself what Addison borrows from his classical mentors. Both seek to convey some image of foreign lands, but Mrs. Radcliffe tries personally to kindle enthusiasm in her readers, a goal that scarcely would have been appreciated by the rationalistic Addison.

In spite of their reliance on the language of poetry and painting, such descriptions suffer inherent limitations: in repeating the same images over and over, they easily tire the reader. To avoid these problems, a book like Mrs. Radcliffe's *Journey* would require "the mutual aid" of the writing pen and the drawing pencil to provide complementary descriptions and illustrations.[69] By relying on words alone, Mrs. Radcliffe competes with those picturesque travelers who actually painted the scenes they witnessed. But even the precise illustrations of these painting travelers are scarcely a return to the factual objectivity that characterizes the accounts of the earlier part of the century. By picturing natural beauty not as it is but as it ought to be, these new illustrators convey an idealized and subjective view of the nature they observe.

William Gilpin, inventor of this "new class of travels," codified his theories in an essay "On Picturesque Travel" (1792), the most influential eighteenth-century statement about travel in search of the beauties of nature. Recognizing the existence of more useful kinds of travel, Gilpin nevertheless classifies picturesque travel as a form

Figure 4. William Gilpin's aquatint of Tintern Abbey, facing p. 45 of his *Observations on the River Wye* (London, 1782).

of "rational amusement" in which the traveler feels rather than surveys the natural setting around him. To this extent, Gilpin's statements echo those of Brydone some twenty years earlier. But Gilpin only suggests how the picturesque traveler should sketch nature with his paint brush; he does not recommend literary techniques that would capture the beauty of nature with words.[70] In his travel accounts Gilpin therefore relies heavily on his own drawings to convey picturesque beauty to his readers. As a result of his "absolute command of Light and Shade," his etchings "represent only the general effect" of the landscape (see fig. 4). They seek to make us feel the way he felt without causing us to see precisely what he saw. While his pictures almost always incited praise, his diction — often larded with terms borrowed from painting — provoked the harsh censure of Thomas Mathias:

I am under the necessity of making a strong remonstrance against *the language* of Mr. Gilpin's writings on landscape and the picturesque. It is such a *sartago* or jargon of speech as is wholly unnecessary, though we are taught to believe them appropriate terms. They absolutely appear in troops. *Dips—Boles—Grand Masses—Belts—tremulous Shudders—Bursts —plashy Inundations—Partitions of Desolation—Contents of Precipice—* and a hundred more, till the English language sets all English meaning at defiance.[71]

Attacks like these, however, were forcefully outweighed by the critical praise that Gilpin earned for his ability to make readers experience natural beauty. Fanny Burney, for example, declared that he showed her "landscapes of every sort, with tints so bright and lively" that she forgot she was reading and fancied she saw them before her. And the *Annual Register* in a similar vein proclaimed that Gilpin united the skill of the artist in sketching objects with the taste of the writer in his verbal delineation of beauty.[72]

Gilpin's imitators, most especially Samuel Ireland and John Hassell, fared considerably less well at the hands of the critics. While their attempts to find and sketch picturesque objects often evoked praise from readers, their verbal skills often seemed inadequate. Ireland's *Picturesque Tour through Holland, Brabant, and Part of France* (1790), for example, inspired the *Monthly Review* to comment negatively on his description of the high road near London:

The flatness of the country renders this scenery less picturesque than that of the Northern or Western outlets from the capital. There is not much to strike the eye of the traveller in the first stage, unless it is the mansion of the Tylney family, on the left of Illford; which is a noble edifice, built from a design of Colin Campbell, and rises, with a degree of magnificence, amidst a thicket of trees in the Forest of Epping. The apartments are spacious; but the pictures, being chiefly family portraits by modern masters, will afford but little entertainment to the connoisseur. In Writtle Park is a handsome modern house, the seat of Lord Petre. The manor on which it stands was a grant by Henry the Eighth, on the dissolution of Barking Abbey.

The *Monthly Review* felt this passage "raised a smile at the expence of the author" since, "in imitation perhaps of Mr. Gilpin's manner," Ireland is much too minute in his descriptions.[73] The *Gentleman's*

*Magazine* was even more severe with John Hassell, quoting the following passage from his *Tour of the Isle of Wight* (1790): "A range of woods, declining from the sight, *rushed* down the mountain's side, to *taste* the river's flow, and join the bending poplar's *nod,* that overhung the beachy clift, and, *unconscious of their charms, in sweet confusion* spread along the basis of the mountains, *to ease the line* of many a rugged step." Labeling this passage "flimsy sublime," the reviewer then asks, "Gentle reader! dost thou really understand all this?"[74] Even worse than the reliance on the pathetic fallacy was the picturesque traveler's use of neologisms; as the reviewer for the *Gentleman's Magazine* pointed out, "the English lexicographer will never want new words, or new senses of words, while picturesque travellers write."[75]

The verbal problems of these picturesque tourists reflect, nevertheless, the inevitable dilemma of every traveler: language rarely conveys an adequately factual or evocative impression of visual objects. Complaining about his inability to describe Fort George, Dr. Johnson distinguishes between scientific descriptions, such as measurements of walls, and "loose and popular" descriptions, such as are employed "only when the imagination is to be amused." Neither of these satisfies Johnson, who dismisses the fort simply by saying that it had "an appearance of the utmost neatness and regularity."[76] The use of aquatints in picturesque travel accounts hence serves as an attempt to supplement verbal descriptions. But in the eyes of contemporary readers, the pictures cannot compensate for faulty words. The travel writer, as a consequence, must demonstrate a writing style commensurate with his painting ability.

Spurred on at least in part by curiosity, that "first and simplest emotion...in the human mind,"[77] eighteenth-century travelers gradually exhausted the most important kinds of information, turning their attention finally to ornamental subjects that demanded increasingly more difficult descriptive techniques. In the process, their descriptions became more ambitious and subjective, moving from lists of factual information to philosophical evaluations of national manners and, finally, to imaginative evocations of natural beauty. Though travel accounts may indeed reflect some shift in the century's aesthetic sensibility concerning the beauties of nature, they more clearly demonstrate a change in the manner in which the century looked at voyages and travels as a literary form. After exhausting useful subjects, the demand for novelty at least in part drove the traveler to describe merely entertaining matters, ultimately changing the fundamental characteristics of a genre that, until the last decades of the century, had uniformly aimed at blending pleasure with useful instruction.

### Reflections: Thoughts Occasioned by What the Traveler Saw

By reflecting on the moral, political, economic, or cultural implications of various foreign and domestic scenes, the eighteenth-century traveler often characterized himself as a philosophic, splenetic, or sentimental traveler without resorting to detailed autobiographical narratives. But since reflections—like aquatints—do not form an essential part of every travel book,[78] the amount of space devoted to such matters varies greatly from one account to another. Nevertheless, the traveler who chose to include reflections usually strove for four essential qualities: his opinions should not be too numerous, they should arise naturally out of the places described, they should be original, and they should not prejudicially conflict with accepted moral or political opinions.

As Coriat Junior observes, readers scarcely "give a penny" for travel accounts "stuffed with the writer's private sentiments and reflections." To support Coriat's observations, we need only turn to the nearly universal condemnation of Jonas Hanway's extravagantly reflective *Journal of Eight Days Journey from Portsmouth to Kingston-upon-Thames.* Dr. Johnson, for example, explains that "it imports little which part" of Hanway's book is read first, since "digression starts from digression, and one subject follows another with or without connexion." In a no more flattering fashion, Goldsmith points out that Hanway indulges in reflections so often that his travels "may with more propriety be stiled *Essays,* or *Meditations.*" By remaining "perpetually upon the watch for an opportunity to introduce . . . his reflections," Hanway ignores "the productions of nature or of art . . . which, one might naturally have imagin'd, would engage his principle attention."[79] In refusing to describe such objects, he inevitably violates the fundamental generic rules of travel literature.

Hanway not only employs too many reflections, but he also introduces them in outrageously awkward fashions. "Any thing serves . . . as a handle" to bring in his philosophical thoughts, enabling him to take every opportunity "to indulge his propensity to moralizing." He describes the inn at Widgate, for instance, simply by saying that it "was not of the most elegant kind." But this brief sentence enables him to launch into a lengthy dissertation on the virtues of temperance. In an even more awkward fashion, he introduces other moral topics by recalling conversations while traveling. Remarking that "our first subject, on the road, was the *vanity* and folly of mankind," he leads his reader into a fourteen-page sermon on this vice, which he then uses to introduce another sermon by saying, "From the consideration whether life is *vain,* we are led to the contemplation of his existence who is the *divine author* of it, and has made *nothing in vain.*"[80] Such an unnatural method of introducing reflections openly invited Paterson's satiric laughter in *Another Traveller!,* where chapter eleven is titled "*A few affecting Twitches, which, it is to be hoped, arise naturally out of the Subject.*"

Reflections moreover must contain "sufficient originality and ingenuity to merit public attention." On these grounds, Hanway's *Journal* once again becomes a prime offender against eighteenth-century literary sensibilities, encouraging the same kinds of criticism leveled by *A Table of all the Accurate Remarks and new Discoveries, in . . . Mr. Addison's Book of Travels.* "Truths which every mortal is . . . well acquainted with" have no place in travel accounts. Thus the "trite and vulgar topics of morality" with which Hanway loaded his *Journal,* though just, make his book "extremely insipid." "Full of trite remarks," Hanway's travel account is much like William Hunter's *Travels in the Year 1792 through France, Turkey, and Hungary, to Vienna* (1796), which lacks "the strength of originality" in its reflections.[81]

Finally, reflections should not prejudicially conflict with currently accepted moral or political opinions. Brydone's otherwise universally praised *Tour,* for example, raised the critical ire of readers when it concluded from the layers of lava on the side of Mount Etna that the world was much older than Archbishop Ussher had calculated. For this reason, Brydone impiously suggests that "Moses hangs like a dead weight . . . and blunts all . . . zeal for inquiry." Boswell and Johnson both took exception to this "antimosaical" reflection, Johnson opining that Brydone would have been a better travel writer if he had been "more attentive to his Bible."[82] Giuseppe Baretti's reflections, written according to the *Critical Review* by "a poor moralist, and a worse politician," incited even more vehement responses among readers. As a foreigner, he understandably was more apt than Brydone to offend the sensibilities of Englishmen. When hazarding the unfashionable opinions that man is naturally cruel and that the English constitution causes evil effects among the populace, Baretti's reflections raised the self-righteous indignation of one reviewer: "Men of the most generous and enlightened minds entertain ill-grounded prejudices in favour of their own country, which no length of time can eradicate." As a consequence, the *Critical Review* found "it in some degree incumbent" upon itself to challenge Baretti's "notions of government, lest they should make some impression upon superficial and inattentive minds." Undoubtedly in order to avoid such attacks, Andrew Burnaby prefaced his *Travels through the Middle Settlements in North America* with an emphatic claim that "party motive" had not influenced him whatsoever when describing the current political conflicts between Great Britain and her American colonies. Yet this loyalist Anglican clergyman nevertheless boldly reflects at the end of his account that the colonies, even if they maintain 100,000 men constantly in arms, cannot withstand the ravages of a mere half dozen English frigates, which with ease would "lay waste the whole country from end to end, without a possibility of their being able to prevent it." With this so-called unprejudiced opinion, Burnaby had little fear of offending the politics of a large majority of his English readers.[83]

Until the advent of the picturesque traveler toward the end of the century, the distinction between "objective" observations and "subjective" reflections remained one of the critical verities of the genre, confidently enabling reviewers, for example, to praise Frederik Hasselquist's *Voyages and Travels in the Levant* (Swedish 1757; English 1766) for describing exactly what the author saw while damning Hanway's *Journal* for its reflective excesses.[84] But when the traveler began describing the beauties of nature, this fundamental distinction necessarily became blurred. In his desire to communicate as entire as possible the impression he received in various natural settings, Brydone describes Mount Etna with largely subjective terms. His observation is itself a form of reflection, his words showing not what the mountain is like, but how it struck him emotionally. In seizing the reader's imagination, Brydone's description conveys the kind of conclusion travelers like Addison would have tried to express through reasoned arguments. Hence when Brydone departs Sicily, his description of the sounds at sea sums up his feelings about the country as a whole.[85]

Following Brydone's lead, picturesque tourists like Gilpin and his imitators turned more and more exclusively to the beauties of nature while relying less and less on conventional reflections about such "important" matters as commerce and politics. In the process, they blurred the distinction between observation and reflection even more than Brydone had done. Frequently, the picturesque tourist employs Brydone's technique of describing natural settings in subjective terms. Thus Joseph Hucks, who visited the rural scenes of Wales on a pedestrian tour with Coleridge during the summer of 1794, conveys the beauty of the landscape with emotionally evocative terms:

The face of the country now became more interesting. The scene gradually assumed a less rugged appearance; the dark brown mountain, and the desolated heath, softened by distance, formed a beautiful contrast to the wild and irregular scenery that succeeded. We felt our spirits, which had before been depressed from the barren and gloomy country we had traversed, now much exhilarated, and we seemed to breathe a freer air.

And Hassell can overdo such evocative descriptions by lapsing into passages loaded with "flimsy sublime": "All the forest of Hampshire was clothed in its wonted splendor. The sun, now gradually declining the hill, launched its glorious hues to the extensive fertile valley

that lay below." But the picturesque tourist often goes one step farther, criticizing the landscape as an art critic would rather than exclusively describing it either in terms of its visual properties or the
emotions that it should elicit from the viewer. Thus Tintern Abbey
comes under Gilpin's censure: "Tho the parts are beautiful, the
whole is ill-shaped. No ruins of the tower are left, which might give
form, and contrast to the buttresses, and walls. Instead of this, a
number of gabel-ends hurt the eye with their regularity; and disgust
it by the vulgarity of their shape."[86] Following the rules of painting,
Gilpin then supplies aquatints that show how various landscapes
should appear (see fig. 4). His observations hence often convey only
opinions, not factual descriptions, and his illustrations perplex those
people who have seen the places he draws.[87]

Such picturesque descriptions in travel literature found important parallels in other literary forms, playing their part in the development of the romantic sensibility. Much romantic poetry, for
example, attempts to convey the impression of having been composed on the spot at a particular time. Thus Wordsworth's poetic
picture of the region near Tintern Abbey, perhaps inspired by Gilpin's similar description some fifteen years earlier, bears the unwieldly title: "Lines Written a Few Miles above Tintern Abbey, on
Revisiting the Banks of the Wye during a Tour, July 13, 1798." In a
less obvious fashion, other romantic poems like Shelley's "Mont
Blanc" stress this kind of immediacy simply by placing dates within
their subtitles. Thus, while Matthew Arnold could characterize
eighteenth-century poetry as having been composed by men "without their eye on the object,"[88] neither romantic poetry nor the eighteenth-century travel account demonstrates that their authors were
anywhere but at the locations described. And by using "particular
nature," descriptive poetry of the romantic period shares the subject
matter often found in eighteenth-century travel books. Finally, and
perhaps most important, the shift to subjective descriptions in travel
books of the eighteenth century points directly toward the "spontaneous overflow of powerful feeling" for which the romantic poet was
soon to aim.

Ultimately we cannot ask when the traveler—or the poet—first looked "with emotion at scenery."[89] Only by ignoring "the peculiarly literary value of literary works"[90] can we assume that the relatively few descriptions of natural settings in early eighteenth-century travel books necessarily reflect their authors' inability to appreciate such beauty. The generic demands of his form forced the traveler first to ignore natural beauty when describing more important subjects. Only when his readers' appetites for encyclopedic information and discussions of foreign manners and customs had been satiated did the quest for novelty press on him a new subject. Thus, in describing picturesque beauty, the eighteenth-century travel writer largely responded to the conventional demands of his genre, demands that were not necessarily dictated by a pervasive change in the century's aesthetic taste.

# CONCLUSION

By commenting that "Dr. Burney's elegant and entertaining travels" were "in his eye" while writing *A Journey to the Western Islands of Soctland,* Dr. Johnson led at least one nineteenth-century reader to suspect that the Rambler "must have skipped widely" in reading his friend's two famous travel books. After all, that "clever dog" Burney writes primarily about music, a topic scarcely mentioned by Johnson.[1] But such a conclusion only reflects the tendency of the nineteenth and twentieth centuries to misunderstand the formal characteristics of eighteenth-century travel literature. While treating different subjects, Johnson's *Journey* and Burney's two tours closely follow the same generic pattern. All three books handle the autobiographical narratives of their author's experiences in the conventional eighteenth-century manner: such personal information simply orders the descriptions, interjects entertainment, and establishes the traveler's character as an accurate, truthful, and perceptive observer. Similarly, each of these travel accounts contains a judicious mixture of observations and reflections in which the reflections seem to derive naturally, by means of an association of ideas, from the observations. In describing Scotland on the one hand and the Continent on the other, each travel writer carefully selects his descriptions, primarily supplying only such information as cannot be found in other travel books. In order to examine its manners and customs, Johnson visited a part of Scotland rarely described in print. And Burney, though traveling through countries that had often been examined, concentrated on music, a subject that had not previously been broached in other travels. Indeed, the titles of Burney's books clearly stress his novel contribution: *The Present State of Music in France and Italy; or, The Journal of a Tour through Those Coun-*

116

*tries* (1771) and *The Present State of Music in Germany, the Nether-lands, and United Provinces; or, The Journal of a Tour through Those Countries* (1773). Hence the travel accounts of Johnson and Burney bear a formal similarity that entirely outweighs their super-ficial differences in subject matter.

Perhaps modern scholarship has failed to understand eighteenth-century travel literature because it expects to find in it the same sort of subjects that characterize the accounts of more recent travelers. For over a century we have tended to think of travel literature as a miscellaneous form of writing primarily governed by the subjective whims of its authors. Hence Walter Scott finds it odd that John Dry-den's son omits from his posthumously published *Voyage to Sicily and Malta* (1776) personal information about the death of his fa-mous father. And Patrick Anderson, explaining that "almost all the best travel-writing is personal," is typical of the kind of twentieth-century reader who finds Johnson's *Journey* less entertaining than Boswell's *Journal of a Tour to the Hebrides* (1785).[2] But modern travels differ markedly from their eighteenth-century ancestors: they tend to be much more autobiographical, and they frequently aim primarily at entertainment. Thus a travel account like *Travels with Charley* is so heavily autobiographical that eighteenth-century reviewers would surely have branded John Steinbeck an "egotist." And Hermann Keyserling's *Travel Diary of a Philosopher* (German 1919; English 1925) begins with a claim that it "should be read like a novel," the kind of assertion that would have thrown John Moore into even graver trouble with his reviewers.[3] Thus when modern readers find Johnson's *Journey* "disappointing"[4] in comparison with Boswell's *Tour to the Hebrides,* they unwittingly yoke together travel accounts with strikingly dissimilar objectives. Johnson defines the controlling aim of his work in a final paragraph: "Such are the things which this journey has given me an opportunity of seeing, and such are the reflections which the sight has raised." In contrast, Boswell explains that his *Tour to the Hebrides* has basically been "the means of preserving so much of the enlightened and instructive conversation of one [i.e., Johnson] whose virtues will . . . ever be an object of imitation, and whose powers of mind were so extraordi-nary, that ages may revolve before such a man shall again appear."[5]

Thus Johnson's book is about Scotland while Boswell's is about Scotland *and* Dr. Johnson. Boswell's account is certainly more anecdotal than Johnson's, but Boswell's anecdotes are largely focused on his famous companion. In this respect, *The Journal of a Tour to the Hebrides with Samuel Johnson* is not unlike Henry Joutel's *Journal of the Last Voyage Perform'd by Monsr. de la Sale* (French 1713; English 1714), which speaks as much about La Salle as it does about the Mississippi basin.

As we have seen, radical changes in eighteenth-century travel literature began occurring toward the end of the century, causing the general outlines of the modern travel book, if only gradually, to emerge: some travel books like John Lettice's *Letters on a Tour through Various Parts of Scotland* became strikingly autobiographical, and others like William Gilpin's *Observations Relative Chiefly to Picturesque Beauty...in...Cumberland and Westmoreland* (1786) aimed at purely entertaining descriptions of nature.[6] But the average travel account during the century is neither fundamentally autobiographical nor primarily aimed at entertaining its readers.

The descriptive and narrative changes were technically related to each other. The descriptive innovations of Patrick Brydone and his followers in part arose from experimentation with novel and progressively more difficult kinds of description. In turn, these innovations necessitated a new autobiographical and fictional emphasis in travel books. Brydone's attempt to seize the reader's imagination and to carry it with him on his tour inevitably forced him to include — if only to a limited, critically acceptable extent — more autobiographical and fictional material than had his predecessors. Though Brydone avoids the trap of "egotism" into which many of his contemporaries fell, his descriptions still convey very personal information about how he felt, and his book thus becomes highly autobiographical. Brydone also employs descriptions in situations that seem fictional, but as Alexander Gerard explained in 1780, "Poetical description" renders "the idea excited by it, livelier and more affecting than that which is produced by a mere narration of facts, by an exact and minute delineation of a natural object." Even though an author — in this case, Brydone — "chuses a real thing for his object," his "description may, notwithstanding, be poetical" to the extent that it is, like fiction, "embellished and enlivened by images" formed in the author's fancy.[7]

Hence when treating natural settings, travelers toward the end of the century often seem more like poets than geographers or philosophers. Their descriptions are no less valid or valuable than those borrowed by Addison from the classical poets, but they now derive from the imagination of the traveler, reflecting how he personally felt in foreign settings. Addison might escape censure in some quarters for his borrowed use of fancy, but travelers following Brydone's lead were often accused of imaginatively shading their pictures of nature "at the expense of . . . accuracy."[8] Only with the introduction of these evocative descriptions did eighteenth-century travel literature finally contain anything like the "emotions recollected in tranquillity" supposedly found in Addison's *Remarks on Italy.*[9]

Until the last decades of the century, travel accounts uniformly aimed at conveying pleasurable instruction, not about the traveler but about the countries he visited. They provided "a pleasing relaxation from severer pursuits," thus enticing "the philosopher and moralist, from solitary and pensive reflection, to the observation of manners and customs." But most important, travel accounts amused "the mind without any degradation from its dignity," exhibiting "a picture, in the contemplation of which, the most fastidious may be usefully exercised, and the most accomplished improved."[10] In avoiding the least appearance of fiction or egotism, they responded to the thirst for facts by a philosophical age, making travel for the sake of education, even into the farthest corners of the world, available to any man who could afford the price of a book.

# ABBREVIATIONS USED IN REFERENCES

AR            *Analytical Review*
CR            *Critical Review*
DNB           *Dictionary of National Biography*
EIC           *Essays in Criticism*
ELN           *English Language Notes*
GM            *Gentleman's Magazine*
LC            *London Chronicle*
LM            *London Magazine*
MLN           *Modern Language Notes*
MP            *Modern Philology*
MLQ           *Modern Language Quarterly*
MR            *Monthly Review*
N&Q           *Notes and Queries*
PBSA          *Papers of the Bibliographical Society of America*
PQ            *Philological Quarterly*
PR            *Political Register*
SM            *Scots Magazine*
SP            *Studies in Philology*
UM            *Universal Magazine*

# NOTES

## INTRODUCTION

1. *Tatler* 254; "Preface by the Editor," *Travels of Carl Philipp Moritz in England in 1782* (1795), intro. P. E. Matheson (London: H. Milford, 1926), p. 3.

2. *MR* 38 (1768), 174; 48 (1772), 199; *CR* 31 (1771), 119. For similar comments, see *AR* 8 (1790), 154, 160; *CR* 1 (1756), 309-310; 20 (1765), 279; 30 (1770), 195-196; 32 (1771), 143; 34 (1772), 130; 41 (1776), 355; 43 (1777), 399; 48 (1779), 208; 68 (1789), 44; 2d ser., 23 (1798), 449; 27 (1799), 481; *GM* 60 (1790), 742; *MR* 38 (1768), 447; 39 (1768), 434-435; 43 (1770), 259; 44 (1771), 396; 46 (1772), 56; 48 (1773), 418; 57 (1777), 207; *UM* 103 (1798), 338.

3. Percy G. Adams, *Travelers and Travel Liars: 1660-1800* (Berkeley and Los Angeles: University of California Press, 1962), p. 224; Jane Austen, *Northanger Abbey,* chap. 14; Frank E. Manuel, *The Eighteenth Century Confronts the Gods* (New York: Atheneum, 1967), passim.

4. According to Paul Kaufman, these two works were the most popular in the Bristol Library (*Borrowings from the Bristol Library: 1773-1784* [Charlottesville: Bibliographical Society of the University of Virginia, 1960], p. 122). On the basis of Kaufman's figures, I have calculated that books dealing with subjects other than travel circulated on an average of slightly less than fourteen times during this period while travel books circulated on an average of slightly more than thirty-two times.

5. See *A Catalogue of the Valuable Library of the Late Celebrated Right Hon. Joseph Addison* (London: [Sotheby and Leigh], 1799); Hilbert H. Campbell, "The Sale Catalogue of Addison's Library," *ELN* 4 (1967), 269-273; John Harrison and Peter Laslett, *The Library of John Locke,* Oxford Bibliographical Society Publications, new ser., 12 (Oxford: Oxford University Press, 1965), 18; Thomas Jemielity, "Dr. Johnson and the Uses of Travel," *PQ* 51 (1972), 449-450 n. 4; *The Letters of David Hume,* ed. J. Y. T. Greig (Oxford: Clarendon Press, 1932), passim; John Pinkerton,

*Modern Geography* (London: T. Cadell, Jun., 1802), I, v; *Catalogue of the Library of Thomas Jefferson,* comp. E. Millicent Sowerby (Washington: Library of Congress, 1952-1959), IV, 85-356. For additional discussions of the popularity and influence of travel literature during the eighteenth century, see James M. Osborn, "Travel Literature and the Rise of Neo-Hellenism in England," in *Literature as a Mode of Travel,* intro. Warner G. Rice (New York: New York Public Library, 1963), pp. 31-52; Paul Fussell, Jr., "Patrick Brydone: The Eighteenth-Century Traveler as Representative Man," *Literature as a Mode of Travel,* pp. 53-67; Adams, *Travelers,* pp. 223-237; G. R. Crone and R. A. Skelton, "English Collections of Voyages and Travels: 1625-1846," in *Richard Hakluyt & His Successors: A Volume Issued to Commemorate the Centenary of the Hakluyt Society,* ed. Edward Lynam (London: Hakluyt Society, 1946), pp. 65-140; Ray W. Frantz, *The English Traveller and the Movement of Ideas, 1660-1732* (1934; Lincoln: University of Nebraska Press, 1967). According to J. H. Plumb, "the output of travel books" during the 1720s and 1730s "was second only to theology" (*England in the Eighteenth Century* [Baltimore: Penguin Books, 1963], p. 30). For the extensive popularity of Dr. John Moore's travel books, see Henry L. Fulton, "An Eighteenth-Century Best Seller," *PBSA* 66 (1972), 428-433.

6. Robert Gray, *Letters During the Course of a Tour through Germany, Switzerland and Italy* (London: F. and C. Rivington, 1794), p. vi; William Mavor, *Historical Account of the Most Celebrated Voyages, Travels, and Discoveries* (London: E. Newbery, 1796-1797), I, A4$^r$.

7. Walpole cited in Paul Franklin Kirby, *The Grand Tour in Italy: 1700-1800* (New York: S. F. Vanni, 1952), p. 8; [James or John James Rutledge], *The Englishman's Fortnight in Paris* (London: T. Durham, 1777), p. i. Concerning the improvements in travel conditions, see William Edward Mead, *The Grand Tour in the Eighteenth Century* (Boston: Houghton Mifflin, 1914), Chaps. IV-VI; E. S. Bates, *Touring in 1600* (Boston: Houghton Mifflin, 1912); Hermann Schreiber, *Merchants, Pilgrims and Highwaymen: A History of Roads through the Ages* (New York: G. P. Putnam's Sons, 1962).

8. Rosamond Bayne-Powell, *Travellers in Eighteenth-Century England* (London: J. Murray, 1951), p. xi. For similar works, see Mead, *Grand Tour;* Constantia Maxwell, *The English Traveller in France, 1698-1815* (London: G. Routledge & Sons, 1932); R. S. Lambert, ed., *The Grand Tour: A Journey in the Tracks of the Age of Aristocracy* (New York: E. P. Dutton, 1937); Kirby, *Grand Tour.*

9. George B. Parks, "The Turn to the Romantic in the Travel Literature of the Eighteenth Century," *MLQ* 25 (1964), 22-33.

10. See Paul Bowles, "Travel: The Challenge to Identity," *Nation* 186 (1958), 360-362.

11. *The Journal of a Tour to the Hebrides, with Samuel Johnson, LL.D.* in *Boswell's Life of Johnson together with Boswell's Journal of a Tour to the Hebrides and Johnson's Diary of a Journey into North Wales*, ed. George Birkbeck Hill and L. F. Powell (Oxford: Clarendon Press, 1934-1950), V, 219; Parks, "Turn to the Romantic," p. 24. Also see an earlier reference in Boswell's *Tour to the Hebrides*, p. 173. For one of Boswell's infrequent attempts at describing natural beauty, see *An Account of Corsica, the Journal of a Tour to That Island, and Memoirs of Pascal Paoli*, 3d ed. (London: E. and C. Dilly, 1769), p. 296.

12. Henri M. Peyre, "Nonfiction Prose Literature," *The New Encyclopaedia Britannica*, 15th ed., Macropaedia, X, 1085; F. A. Kirkpatrick, "The Literature of Travel, 1700-1900," in *The Cambridge History of English Literature*, ed. A. W. Ward and A. R. Waller (New York: G. P. Putnam's Sons, 1907-1917), Vol. XIV, part iii, p. 265.

13. Nathaniel Wraxall, *Cursory Remarks*, printed as *A Tour round the Baltic through the Northern Countries of Europe*, 4th ed. (London: T. Cadell, 1807), p. 3. For Johnson's similar distinction between ancient and modern travelers, see Boswell, *Life of Johnson*, III, 356.

14. *CR* 27 (1769), 52; Anthony Ashley Cooper, third earl of Shaftesbury, *Characteristics of Men, Manners, Opinions, Times, Etc.*, ed. John M. Robertson (London: G. Richards, 1900), I, 223.

15. W. T. Jewkes, "The Literature of Travel and the Mode of Romance in the Renaissance," in *Literature as a Mode of Travel*, pp. 15-16; *Othello*, I, iii, 128-145; Joseph Hall, *Virgidemiarum*, IV, vi, 58, in *The Collected Poems of Joseph Hall*, ed. A. Davenport (Liverpool: University Press, 1949), p. 71. Also see Thomas B. Stroup, "Shakespeare's Use of a Travelbook Commonplace," *PQ* 17 (1938), 351-358.

16. Shaftesbury, *Characteristics*, I, 222-223; William White, "The Narrative Technique of Elizabethan Voyage and Travel Literature from 1550 to 1603," *Dissertation Abstracts* 15 (1955), 1622. For a discussion of the nonliterary nature of these works, see White, "Narrative Technique," (Diss. Lehigh University 1955), pp. 21, 279-281.

17. William Guthrie, *A New System of Modern Geography*, 4th ed. (London: C. Dilly, 1788), p. vi.

18. Jeffrey Hart, "Johnson's *A Journey to the Western Islands:* History as Art," *EIC* 10 (1960), 44-45; Hans-Joachim Possin, *Reisen und Literatur: Das Thema des Reisens in der englischen Literatur des 18. Jahrhunderts* (Tübingen: M. Niemeyer, 1972), p. 258.

19. Michel Adanson, *A Voyage to Senegal* (London: J. Nourse, 1759),

pp. iii-iv [fonts reversed]. Also see [Jean Baptiste Morvan de Bellegarde], *A General History of All Voyages and Travels* (London: E. Curll, 1708), p. 32.

20. Joseph Pitts, *A True and Faithful Account of the Religion and Manners of the Mohammetans* (Exeter: P. Bishop, 1704), A5$^r$ [fonts reversed].

21. Anders Sparrman, *A Voyage to the Cape of Good Hope* (London: G. G. J. and J. Robinson, 1785), I, iii-iv.


## I. TOWARD A DEFINITION

1. *The Letters of Joseph Addison,* ed. Walter Graham (Oxford: Clarendon Press, 1941), p. 4; John Locke, *Some Thoughts concerning Education* (1693), in *The Educational Writings of John Locke,* ed. James L. Axtell (Cambridge: Cambridge University Press, 1968), pp. 321-323.

2. English editions of *Remarks on Several Parts of Italy, &c.: In the Years 1701, 1702, 1703* appeared in 1705, 1718, 1726, 1733, 1736, 1745, 1753, 1755 (Glasgow), 1761, 1762, 1767, 1769 (n.p.), 1773 (Dublin). A French translation served as volume 4 of Maximilien Misson's *Nouveau voyage d'Italie,* 5th ed. (1722); the Dutch translation appeared as volume 4 of Misson's *Nieuwe reize van Misson na en door Italien* (1724).

3. Also see Addison's *Remarks* in Edward Cavendish Drake's *New Universal Collection of Authentic and Entertaining Voyages and Travels* (1768) and John Hamilton Moore's *New and Complete Collection of Voyages and Travels* (1780?). Even in the twentieth century, *Remarks on Italy* found its way into Francis W. Halsey's *Seeing Europe with Famous Authors* (New York: Funk and Wagnalls, 1914), VII, 10-16; VIII, 69-72.

4. Jean Le Clerc, *Bibliothèque choisie* (Amsterdam: H. Schelte, 1703-1713), XI, 198; *Journal des Sçavans,* supplement (1709), p. 86 [misnumbered p. 89]; John Durant Breval, *Remarks on Several Parts of Europe: Relating Chiefly to the History, Antiquities and Geography, of Those Countries through Which the Author Has Travel'd* (London: B. Lintot, 1726), I, fol. a2$^r$ [fonts reversed]; Henry Fielding, *The Journal of a Voyage to Lisbon,* ed. Harold E. Pagliaro (New York: Nardon Press, 1963), p. 25. Also see *Biographia Britannica* (London: W. Innys, 1747-1766), I, 33.

5. *The Correspondence of James Boswell and John Johnston of Grange,* ed. Ralph S. Walker (London: Heinemann, 1966), pp. 98, 146-147, 178; *Boswell on the Grand Tour: Germany and Switzerland, 1764,* ed. Frederick A. Pottle (New York: McGraw-Hill, 1953), p. 209; *Boswell on the*

*Grand Tour: Italy, Corsica, and France, 1765-66,* ed. Frank Brady and Frederick A. Pottle (New York: McGraw-Hill, 1955), pp. 41-43. For Addison's descriptions of Milan and Soleurre, see *Remarks on Several Parts of Italy, &c.: In the Years 1701, 1702, 1703* in *The Miscellaneous Works of Joseph Addison,* ed. A. C. Guthkelch (London: G. Bell and Sons, 1914), II, 27-40, 213; unless otherwise indicated, all quotations from *Remarks on Italy* will be cited parenthetically within the text, referring to the second volume of this edition.

6. *The Complete Letters of Lady Mary Wortley Montagu,* ed. Robert Halsband (Oxford: Clarendon Press, 1965-1967), I, 331; *Horace Walpole's Correspondence with Thomas Gray, Richard West, and Thomas Ashton,* ed. W. S. Lewis, George L. Lam, and Charles H. Bennett, The Yale Edition of Horace Walpole's Correspondence, Vols. XIII, XIV (New Haven: Yale University Press, 1948), I, 85-90; *Gibbon's Journey from Geneva to Rome,* ed. Georges A. Bonnard (London: T. Nelson and Sons, 1961), pp. 125-126, 130, 135, 224. Also see *The Letters of David Hume,* ed. J. Y. T. Greig (Oxford: Clarendon Press, 1932), II, 44, 374.

7. See, for example, Breval, *Remarks on Several Parts of Europe: Relating Chiefly to the History, Antiquities and Geography,* II, 3, 19-20, 49-52, 63, 98, 101, 124, 133, 137, 171-172, 230, 236, 265-266, 281, 286, 305, 310; Edward Wright, *Some Observations Made in Travelling through France, Italy, &c.* (London: T. Ward, 1730), I, 24, 89, 109, 132, 270; II, 465; Breval, *Remarks on Several Parts of Europe, Relating Chiefly to Their Antiquities and History* (London: H. Lintot, 1738), I, 51, 62, 116, 129, 132, 151-153, 184, 275, 281; Charles Thompson [pseud. ?], *The Travels of the Late Charles Thompson* (Reading: J. Newbery, 1744), I, A3$^r$, 69-70, 80, 82, 91, 101, 116, 118, 125-127, 152-153, 161, 174, 175, 177, 179-180, 188, 190, 192, 199, 200, 212, 215, 224, 227, 228 245, 253; James or John Russell, *Letters from a Young Painter Abroad,* 2d ed. (London: W. Russel, 1750), I, 58, 59, 60, 93, 98, 100, 102, 107, 111; Alexander Drummond, *Travels through Different Cities of Germany, Italy, Greece, and Several Parts of Asia* (London: For the author, 1754), pp. 2, 20, 25, 26, 28, 29, 34, 38, 44, 53, 61, 67, 86, 88; Johann Georg Keyssler, *Travels through Germany, Bohemia, Hungary, Switzerland, Italy, and Lorrain,* 3d ed. (London: G. Keith, 1760), II, 13, 55, 441; III, 19, 117, 134, 175, 176, 400; IV, 4; Samuel Sharp, *Letters from Italy* (London: R. Cave, 1766), pp. 120, 133; Tobias Smollett, *Travels through France and Italy* (1766), intro. James Morris (Fontwell, Sussex: Centaur Press, 1969), pp. 295, 305, 367; Anna Riggs Miller, *Letters from Italy* (London: E. and C. Dilly, 1776), I, 315, 330, 333-337, 339; II, 155-157; Thomas Nugent, *The Grand Tour,* 3d ed.

(London: J. Rivington and Sons, 1778), I, x; John Moore, *A View of Society and Manners in Italy* (London: W. Strahan, 1781), I, 281, 312, 368, 372, 375; Hester Lynch Thrale Piozzi, *Observation and Reflections Made in the Course of a Journey through France, Italy, and Germany* (1789), ed. Herbert Barrows (Ann Arbor: University of Michigan Press, 1967), pp. 39, 71, 138, 257; James Edward Smith, *A Sketch of a Tour on the Continent* (London: J. Davis, 1793), II, 79-80, 300, 302-303; III, 263; Mariana Starke, *Travels in Italy* (London: R. Phillips, 1802), II, 44; John Chetwode Eustace, *A Classical Tour through Italy,* 3d ed. (London: J. Mawman, 1819), I, xxxiv-xxxvi, 183-184, 507-508; Antoine Valery, *Voyages historiques, littéraires et artistiques en Italie,* 2d ed. (Paris: A. André, 1838), I, 39, 437; II, 184, 397, 405, 463.

8. Eustace, *Classical Tour,* I, xxxiv; Paul Franklin Kirby, *The Grand Tour in Italy: 1700-1800* (New York: S. F. Vanni, 1952), p. 6. For further indications of Addison's reputation as a travel writer, see *AR* 15 (1793), 376; Paul R. Baker, *The Fortunate Pilgrims: Americans in Italy, 1800-1860* (Cambridge, Mass.: Harvard University Press, 1964), p. 12; Hans-Joachim Possin, *Reisen und Literatur: Das Thema des Reisens in der englischen Literatur des 18. Jahrhunderts* (Tübingen: M. Niemeyer, 1972), p. 28.

9. See Warton, "Ode to a Gentleman on His Travels" (1748), in *Biographical Memoirs of the Late Revd. Joseph Warton, D.D.,* ed. John Wooll (London: T. Cadell, 1806), pp. 133-136; *The Twickenham Edition of the Poems of Alexander Pope,* ed. John Butt (London: Methuen, 1939-1969), I, 268n; II, 258n. For additional evidence that Pope had read and appreciated Addison's *Remarks on Italy,* see *The Twickenham Edition,* I, 183n, 184n, 226n; II, 163n, 231n, 250n.

10. *A Table of All the Accurate Remarks and New Discoveries, in the Most Learned and Ingenious Mr. Addison's Book of Travels* (London: Company of Long-Bow-String-Makers, 1706), pp. 3, 5; for corresponding statements, see *Remarks,* pp. 183, 217, 229.

11. Thomas Babington Macaulay, "The Life and Writings of Addison," in *Critical and Historical Essays,* comp. A. J. Grieve (London: J. M. Dent, 1907), II, 479; Gosse, "Addison's Travels" (1897), reprinted in *Among My Books,* ed. H. D. Traill (London: E. Stock, [1898?]), p. 54; Bonamy Dobrée, *English Literature in the Early Eighteenth Century,* The Oxford History of English Literature (Oxford: Clarendon, Press, 1945— ), VII, 104. Macaulay seems to translate into nineteenth-century terms Thomas Tickell's statement that initial readers of *Remarks on Italy* expected "an account, in a common way, of the customs and policies of the several govern-

ments in *Italy,* reflexions upon the genius of the people, a map of their provinces, or a measure of their buildings" (*The Works of the Right Honourable Joseph Addison, Esq.,* ed. Thomas Tickell [London: J. Tonson, 1721], I, viii).

12. These quotations come from the following authors: Silius Italicus, 27; Virgil, 24; Claudian, 14; Lucan, 14; Juvenal, 13; Martial, 12; Horace, 10; Ovid, 6; Statius, 4; Ausonius, 3; Sannazaro, 3; Homer, 2; Propertius, 2; Greek epigrammatists, 2; Tibullus, 1; Phaedrus, 1; Manilius, 1; Seneca, 1; unknown, 1. This compilation appears in Clark S. Northup's "Addison and Gray as Travellers," *Studies in Language and Literature in Celebration of the Seventieth Birthday of James Morgan Hart* (New York: H. Holt, 1910), p. 406. Northup furthermore concludes that "in length these quotations range from a part of a line to 35 lines; the average, if we count parts of lines as wholes, is 4.6 lines."

13. *Table,* A2$^\mathrm{r}$. By quoting these two lines of poetry, *A Table* subtly compares Addison with Hudibras, Butler's famous antiroyalist precursor of the Whigs (see *Hudibras,* I, iii, 1009-1012).

14. Horace Walpole, *Correspondence with Gray,* I, 85-90; Laurence Sterne, *The Life and Opinions of Tristram Shandy, Gentleman,* ed. James Aiken Work (New York: Odyssey Press, 1940), pp. 482-483. Likewise see Fielding, *Voyage to Lisbon,* p. 25; *Correspondence of Thomas Gray,* ed. Paget Toynbee and Leonard Whibley (Oxford: Clarendon Press, 1935), I, 379.

15. Dobrée, *English Literature in the Early Eighteenth Century,* pp. 103-104. Harold Routh similarly implies that "enthusiasm" for "ancient literature" guided Addison (*The Cambridge History of English Literature,* ed. A. W. Ward and A. R. Waller [New York: G. P. Putnam's Sons, 1907-1917], IX, 49), and Edward Malins suggests that Addison lacked any interest in contemporary paintings and current events (*English Landscaping and* Literature: 1660-1840 [London: Oxford University Press, 1966], p. 21).

16. *DNB* II, 1198; Pope, *The Dunciad in Four Books,* IV, 327.

17. See Clarence DeWitt Thorpe, "Two Augustans Cross the Alps: Dennis and Addison on Mountain Scenery," *SP* 32 (1935), 463-482, and Donald F. Bond's review or this article in *PQ* 15 (1936), 171-172.

18. For other studies that use this distinction, see Raymond D. Havens, "Romantic Aspects in the Age of Pope," *PMLA* 27 (1912), 297-324; Thomas Sergeant Perry, *English Literature in the Eighteenth Century* (New York: Harper, 1883), pp. 144-148, 393; William Lyon Phelps, *The Beginnings of the English Romantic Movement* (Boston: Ginn, 1893), pp.

166-169; John Addington Symonds, *Sketches and Studies in Italy and Greece*, 1st ser., new ed. (London: J. Murray, 1914), p. 3; Hans-Joachim Possin, *Natur und Landschaft bei Addison* (Tübingen: M. Niemeyer, 1965), passim.

19. Marjorie Hope Nicolson, *Mountain Gloom and Mountain Glory: The Development of the Aesthetics of the Infinite* (Ithaca: Cornell University Press, 1959), pp. 1, 3.

20. Ibid., p. 19, citing Myra Reynolds, *The Treatment of Nature in English Poetry* (1907). As Jean Hagstrum has pointed out, Nicolson ignores the landscapes of Titian, Tintoretto, Salvator Rosa, and Magnasco. Moreover, she fails to consider "Ovid's 'sympathetic' landscapes, Shakespeare's dramatic use of wild nature in the tragedies, Ariosto's desolate Alpine scenes" together with "Vasari's and E.K.'s delight in 'naturall rudeness' and 'disorderly order.'" all of which antedate the eighteenth century (see Hagstrum's review of *Mountain Gloom* in *MLN* 76 [1961], 50). Nicolson perhaps should also have taken into account poems like Shakespeare's Sonnet 33.

21. Joshua Poole, *The English Parnassus: Or a Help to English Poesie* (London: H. Brome, 1677), p. 129, cited in part in Nicolson, *Mountain Gloom*, p. 35; John Livingston Lowes, *The Road to Xanadu: A Study in the Ways of the Imagination* (New York: Vintage Books, 1959), p. 290; John Evelyn, *Diary* (ca. May 1646), cited in *Mountain Gloom*, p. 62; Thomas Hobbes, *De Mirabilibus Pecci Carmen: Being the Wonders of the Peak in Darbyshire* (1678), cited in *Mountain Gloom*, p. 65.

22. Nicolson, *Mountain Gloom*, p. 306.

23. See Addison's *Letters*, p. 30, and *Remarks*, p. 198.

24. *Spectator* 364; Boswell, *The Journal of a Tour to the Hebrides, with Samuel Johnson, LL.D.* in Boswell's *Life of Johnson*, ed. Goerge Birkbeck Hill and L. F. Powell (Oxford: Clarendon Press, 1934-1950), V, 310; *The Miscellaneous Works of Joseph Addison in Four Volumes* (London: Lewis A. Lewis, 1830), I, xv-xvi; *Works of Addison*, ed. Tickell, I, viii-ix. Concerning the authorship and reprinting of the passage praising *Remarks on Italy* in *Spectator* 364, see Donald F. Bond, ed., *The Spectator* (Oxford: Clarendon Press, 1965), III, 366 n. 2; 369 n. 1.

25. Percy G. Adams, *Travelers and Travel Liars: 1660-1800* (Berkeley and Los Angeles: University of California Press, 1962), Chap. I.

26. Young, *Travels in France during the Years 1787, 1788 & 1789*, ed. Constantia Maxwell (Cambridge: Cambridge University Press, 1929), p. 151; Coriat Junior [Samuel Paterson], *Another Traveller! or Cursory Remarks and Tritical Observations Made upon a Journey through Part of the*

*Netherlands in the Latter End of the Year 1766* (London: J. Johnson, 1767-1769), I, 53-54.

27. According to Addison's letters, he was in Marseilles during November 1700, in Venice during January 1700-1701, and in Rome during July and August 1701. *Remarks on Italy* tells us that he traveled from Marseilles to Rome by way of Genoa, Milan, Venice, and Loretto; after a very brief stay in Rome he journeyed to Naples and then returned to Rome for a lengthy visit. If we believe his letters, he must have been in Venice on Holy Thursday (Ascension Day), which fell on 29 May O.S. or 5 May N.S. in 1701. But after leaving Venice he could not have traveled from Loretto to Rome during February, as he reports in his *Remarks,* nor could he have celebrated Easter Week of 1701 in Naples if he had already observed acrobatics in Venice on Holy Thursday, as he reports in his travel account. Other problems with dates appear in *Remarks on Italy.* While its title page implies that Addison's travels took place in 1701, 1702, and 1703, the first chapter begins with his setting out "from *Marseilles* to *Genoa*" on "the twelfth of *December,* 1699." Addison in fact did not leave Marseilles until a year later, in December 1700. Thomas Macaulay, who seems to have been the first person to recognize this inconsistency, observed that Addison's "slip of the pen," which "throws the whole narrative into inextricable confusion," strangely occurs in all editions, never having been detected by Tickell or Hurd, his editors (*Critical and Historical Essays,* II, 469 n. 1). Even more curious is Addison's failure to catch this mistake when revising his *Remarks* in 1718. Similarly, while its title page leads us to believe that *Remarks on Italy* describes Addison's travels during 1703, a glance at his letters shows that by November 1702 he had reached Vienna, a city not yet described by the end of the book.

28. *CR* 30 (1770), 196; for descriptions of the Grotto del Cani, see Maximilien Misson, *Nouveau voyage d'Italie* (The Hague: H. van Bulderen, 1717), III, 246-247; Charles Bourdin, *Voyage d'Italie* (Paderborn: C. Pelerin, 1699), pp. 221-222; *The Travels of the Learned Father Montfaucon from Paris thro' Italy* (London: E. Curll, 1712), pp. 374-375.

29. Jeronymo Lobo, *A Voyage to Abyssinia* (London: A. Bettesworth, 1735), pp. vii-viii.

30. Tobias Smollett, *The Adventures of Ferdinand Count Fathom,* ed. Damian Grant (London: Oxford University Press, 1971), pp. 2-3.

31. Sheldon Sacks, *Fiction and the Shape of Belief: A Study of Henry Fielding with Glances at Swift, Johnson and Richardson* (Berkeley and Los Angeles: University of California Press, 1967), p. 271; B. L. Reid, "Smollett's Healing Journey," *Virginia Quarterly Review* 41 (1965), 550; M. A.

Goldberg, *Smollett and the Scottish School: Studies in Eighteenth-Century Thought* (Albuquerque: University of New Mexico Press, 1959), p. 182. Other critics virtually ignore the non-novelistic elements in *Humphry Clinker;* see, for instance, Tuvia Bloch, "Smollett's Quest for Form," *MP* 65 (1967), 107 n. 13. For Byron Gassman's attempt to resolve this generic problem, see "The Economy of *Humphry Clinker,*" in *Tobias Smollett: Bicentennial Essays Presented to Lewis M. Knapp,* ed. G. S. Rousseau and P.-G. Boucé (New York: Oxford University Press, 1971), p. 157. I answer Gassman's article in *"Humphry Clinker* and Eighteenth-Century Travel Literature," *Genre* 7 (1974), 392-408.

32. Robert Chambers, *Smollett: His Life and a Selection from His Writings* (Edinburgh: W. & R. Chambers, 1867), p. 130.

33. George M. Kahrl, *Tobias Smollett: Traveler-Novelist* (Chicago: University of Chicago Press, 1945), pp. 125-126. Also see Lewis M. Knapp, "Smollett's Self-Portrait in *The Expedition of Humphry Clinker,*" in *The Age of Johnson: Essays Presented to Chauncey Brewster Tinker,* ed. Frederick W. Hilles (New Haven: Yale University Press, 1949), pp. 149-158; Howard Mumford Jones, "Introduction," *The Expedition of Humphry Clinker,* ed. Charles Lee (London: J. M. Dent, 1943), pp. ix-x; George M. Kahrl, "Captain Robert Stobo," *Virginia Magazine of History and Biography* 49 (1941), 141-151, 254-268.

34. *The Letters of Tobias Smollett,* ed. Lewis M. Knapp (Oxford: Clarendon Press, 1970), p. 125; italics mine. Though we know that Smollett, for example, spent the months of September, October, and November, 1764, in Italy, Letters XVIII-XXII in his *Travels,* supposedly written during this time, are all dated from France and describe the city of Nice. Similarly, Smollett describes in Letter XVI a murder he saw in Florence, in spite of the fact that the letter is dated at least two months before he even arrived in Italy (see Kahrl, *Tobias Smollett,* pp. 104-105; Louis Martz, *The Later Career of Tobias Smollett* [New Haven: Yale University Press, 1942], pp. 68-73).

35. Quoted from the title page of the first edition of Smollett's *Travels through France and Italy* (London: R. Baldwin, 1766).

36. Mary Kingsley, quoted by F. A. Kirkpatrick, in *Cambridge History of English Literature,* XIV, pt. iii, 265. Basil D. Nicholson similarly quotes Matthew Arnold as claiming that a travel book simply "exists . . . to get its ends, to make its points" ("Travellers and Their Tales," *Bookman* 82 [1932], 235).

37. René Wellek, *A History of Modern Criticism: 1750-1950* (New Haven: Yale University Press, 1955), I, 21. Concerning *utile dulce,* also see

Marvin T. Herrick, *The Fusion of Horatian and Aristotelian Literary Criticism, 1531-1555* (Urbana: University of Illinois Press, 1946), pp. 39-47; M. H. Abrams, *The Mirror and the Lamp: Romantic Theory and the Critical Tradition* (New York: Oxford University Press, 1953), pp. 14-21.

38. Daniel Beeckman, *A Voyage to and from the Island of Borneo* (London: T. Warner, 1718), A5$^V$; Pascoe Thomas, *A True and Impartial Journal of a Voyage to the South-Seas* (London: S. Birt, 1745), A2$^r$; [N.N.], *Directions for a Proper Choice of Authors to Form a Library* (London: J. Whiston, 1766), p. 20.

39. See Defoe, *A Tour through the Whole Island of Great Britain,* intro. G. D. H. Cole and D. C. Browning (London: J. M. Dent, 1962), I, 1; Horace, *Ars poetica* 343-344; *CR* 46 (1778), 452; George Sherburn and Donald F. Bond, *The Restoration and Eighteenth Century (1660-1789),* in *A Literary History of England,* ed. Albert C. Baugh, 2d ed. (New York: Appleton-Century-Crofts, 1967), p. 850. In professedly implementing Horace's dual functions, Defoe follows a common practice in travel accounts; see, for instance, Drummond, *Travels,* p. 1; [William Thomson, also known as Thomas Newte], *A Tour in England and Scotland* (London: G. G. and J. Robinson, 1788), p. 2. For a discussion of the fictional nature of Defoe's *Tour,* see G. D. H. Cole's "Introduction to the Tour through England and Wales" in *Tour,* I, xv-xvi.

40. Fielding, *Voyage to Lisbon,* p. 23.

41. Ibid., p. 30.

42. *CR* 30 (1770), 195-196; 8 (1759), 487; 1 (1756), 309; 18 (1764), 375-376. Ralph Griffiths similarly says that sea journals, which "are generally looked upon as truth," have "a much stronger claim to the reader's attention, than the most striking incidents in a novel or romance" (*MR* 4 [1750], 63).

43. *CR* 20 (1765), 279; 1 (1756), 309. Also see Vicesimus Knox, *Essays, Moral and Literary,* 5th ed. (London: C. Dilly, 1784), I, 113-118; *SM* 39 (1777), 258.

44. The *Critical Review*'s comment on William Coxe's *Travels in Switzerland* (1789) is typical of the kind of praise accorded travel books that please and instruct a general audience: Coxe's *Travels* "may be considered as valuable additions to the stock of English literature: we can truly say, that we have not for a long time read any work from which we have derived so much entertainment and instruction" (*CR* 68 [1789], 436). For similar comments, see *AR* 8 (1790), 155; *CR* 2 (1756), 363; 25 (1768), 206; 39 (1775), 80; 63 (1787), 478; 2d ser., 18 (1796), 135; 23 (1798), 13; 25 (1799), 311; *GM* 60 (1790), 742, 833; *LC* 26 (1769), 545; 34 (1773), 149; 35

(1774), 449; 49 (1781), 337; 53 (1783), 489; *MR* 4 (1750), 63; 39 (1768), 63; 45 (1771), 561; *SM* 39 (1777), 258; *UM* 89 (1791), 250. Yet the *Critical Review* censured Jonas Hanway's *Journal of Eight Days Journey* (1756) for lacking both these qualities "little entertainment or instruction can be gathered from that extravagant profusion of reflections, with which Mr. H——'s work abounds" (*CR* 4 [1757], 2). For similar comments, see *AR* 9 (1791), 408; *CR* 4 (1757), 371; 41 (1776), 486; 43 (1777), 449; 2d ser., 24 (1798), 455; *MR* 44 (1771), 159.

45. *CR* 38 (1774), 178; 39 (1775), 470, 473.

46. *MR* 43 (1770), 551-552; *AR* 10 (1791), 165. For similar comments, see *CR* 36 (1773), 241-242; 2d ser., 21 (1797), 38-39.

47. *CR* 43 (1777), 280. The reviewer compares Inigo Born's *Travels through the Bannat of Temeswar* with Johann Jakob Ferber's *Travels through Italy* (1776), a work that likewise primarily describes minerals. Ferber, however, fails to entertain readers as Born does (see *Travels,* pp. 169-170). According to the *Analytical Review,* Dr. James Edward Smith's *Sketch of a Tour on the Continent* (1793) demonstrates that even a learned man with specialized botanical interests can write an entertaining account directed at a general reading audience (*AR* 18 [1794], 271-272).

48. Defoe, *Tour,* I, 311; Pope, *Windsor-Forest* (1713); William Gilpin, *Observations on the River Wye, and Several Parts of South Wales,* 5th ed. (London: T. Cadell junior, 1800), p. 1; John Hassell, *Tour of the Isle of Wight* (London: T. Hookham, 1790), I, vi; *Travels of Carl Philipp Moritz in England in 1782,* intro. P. E. Matheson (London: H. Milford, 1926), p. 8.

49. See for instance, Evelyn's use of travel guides in *The Diary of John Evelyn,* ed. E. S. de Beer (Oxford: Clarendon Press, 1955), I, 86-101; II, 214 and n. 1.

50. [Burney], *MR* 2d ser., 32 (1800), 225; *CR* 2d ser., 29 (1800), 198.

51. See William Beckford, *Dreams, Waking Thoughts and Incidents,* ed. Robert J. Gemmett (Rutherford, N.J.: Fairleigh Dickinson University Press, 1971), pp. 25-26.

52. Samuel Johnson, *Rambler* 125. Also see Ralph W. Rader, "The Concept of Genre and Eighteenth-Century Studies," in *New Approaches to Eighteenth-Century Literature: Selected Papers from the English Institute,* ed. Phillip Harth (New York: Columbia University Press, 1974), pp. 79-115.

53. *GM* 25 (1755), 129.

54. See, for example, the title page of G. H. Millar's *New and Universal System of Geography* (London: A. Hogg, 1782). Because of these similari-

ities between eighteenth-century travel literature and other literary forms, George Sherburn classifies travel accounts as "specialized autobiographies," while E. Millicent Sowerby groups them under the heading of "Geography" (Sherburn and Bond, *Restoration and Eighteenth Century*, p. 1067; Sowerby, *Catalogue of the Library of Thomas Jefferson* (Washington: Library of Congress, 1952-1959), IV, 85-356). Bonamy Dobrée hedges on the subject: "If Tours are not strictly speaking diaries or journals, they can plausibly be included among such, since they are for the most part clearly enough derived from jottings taken down from day to day" (Dobrée, *English Literature in the Early Eighteenth Century*, p. 368). Also see E. Stuart Bates, *Inside Out: An Introduction to Autobiography* (New York: Sheridan House, 1937), pp. 4-5; Paul Delany, *British Autobiography in the Seventeenth Century* (London: Routledge, 1969), pp. 116-120; James C. Johnston, *Biography: The Literature of Personality* (New York: Century, 1927), pp. 190-198.

55. *MR* 44 (1771), 396; 51 (1774), 504. Also see Isaac Watts, *Improvement of the Mind* (1741; New York: A. S. Barnes, 1849), p. 46.

56. Young, *Travels in France*, pp. 1-3. In spite of the popularity enjoyed by *Travels in France*, its section entitled General Observations has never been reprinted in full since the eighteenth century. Most editions now, however, reprint the Journal in its entirety (see Editor's Note, *Travels in France*, p. xi). For a similar arrangement of Journal and Observations, see Young's *Six Months Tour through the North of England* (1770).

57. James Boswell, *An Account of Corsica, the Journal of a Tour to that Island, and Memoirs of Pascal Paoli*, 3d ed. (London: E. and C. Dilly, 1769), p. xiv. The "learned friends" perhaps were Lord Hailes and Lord Monboddo (see Frederick A. Pottle, *James Boswell: The Earlier Years, 1740-1769* [New York: McGraw-Hill, 1966], p. 339.

58. Boswell, *Life of Johnson*, II, 70. Johnson's comments echo the *Critical Review*'s statement that "the journal of a tour to Corsica, and memoirs of Pascal Paoli, form the last, and we think most entertaining, division of this work, because it could not be the result of reading or information" (*CR* 25 [1768], 178). Boswell likewise believed his *Journal* formed "the most valuable" part of *An Account of Corsica* (*Letters of James Boswell*, ed. Chauncey Brewster Tinker [Oxford: Clarendon Press, 1924], I, 129).

59. Boswell, *Account of Corsica*, p. xxxi. For additional comments on this kind of organization, see *CR* 27 (1769), 257-259; 38 (1774), 175.

60. Articles by John Symonds, professor of Modern History at Cambridge, appear in *Annals of Agriculture*, ed. Arthur Young, 3 (1785), 15-46, 137-166; 5 (1786), 317-348.

61. *CR* 43 (1777), 426-427; 2d ser., 14 (1795), 171-172; 18 (1796), 493; [Alphonse Marseille de Fortia de Piles and Pierre de Boisgelin de Kerdu], *Voyage de deux Français en Allemagne, Danemarck, Suède, Russie et Pologne* (Paris: Desenne, 1796), I, 1.

62. John Millard, *The Gentleman's Guide in His Tour through France,* 4th ed. (London: G. Kearsly, 1770), p. iii.

63. *AR* 8 (1790), 160.

64. *CR* 48 (1779), 208-209. Note, also, that Pierre Poivre's *Travels of a Philosopher* (1769) and Thomas Shaw's *Travels, or Observations relating to Several Parts of Barbary and the Levant* (1738) are not actually travel books.

65. Fielding, however, confuses the dates in his journal (see *Voyage to Lisbon,* p. 143, n. 78). While Addison does not label his divisions specifically as chapters, he refers to them as such within the body of his work (see, for instance, *Remarks,* pp. 88, 191, 199).

66. William Dalrymple, *Travels through Spain and Portugal* (London: J. Almon, 1777), p. 1. Also see Mrs. Piozzi's comment on why she published her travel book in the form of a journal rather than a collection of letters: "I have not thrown my thoughts into the form of private letters; because a work of which truth is the best recommendation, should not above all others begin with a lie" (*Observations and Reflections,* p. 2).

67. *MR* 45 (1771), 212.

68. *CR* 7 (1759), 505. Concerning the authorship of this review, see Arthur Friedman, "Goldsmith's Contributions to the *Critical Review,*" *MP* 44 (1946), 35.

69. *CR* 22 (1766), 434; 25 (1768), 284; *MR* 45 (1771), 561; *CR* 68 (1789), 108. For similar comments, see *AR* 8 (1790), 155; *CR* 30 (1770), 428; 32 (1771), 179; 35 (1773), 58, 211; 43 (1777), 449; 63 (1787), 476; 2d ser., 21 (1797), 265; *MR* 43 (1770), 551; 44 (1771), 158-162; 48 (1773), 506-507.

70. *CR* 47 (1779), 417. Boswell similarly says that, as a travel writer, he aims at giving readers "a free and continued account" of what he "saw or heard" (*Account of Corsica,* p. 301).

71. John Hawkesworth, *Adventurer* 4; *MR* 53 (1775), 193; Giuseppe Baretti, *A Journey from London to Genoa* (London: T. Davies, 1770), I, vi; *MR* 49 (1773), 23. Also see George Berkeley's *Journal of Travels in Italy* (first printed in 1871), in *The Works of George Berkeley,* ed. A. A. Luce and T. E. Jessop (London: T. Nelson and Sons, 1948-1957), VII, 229-333; *Gibbon's Journey from Geneva to Rome,* passim.

72. *CR* 66 (1788), 70. For the judgment that Pennant's *Tour in Scotland*

is "free from the charge of egotism," see *CR* 33 (1772), 17. The dropping of personal pronouns can also be found in brief periodical travel descriptions such as T. Rambler's "Account of an Excursion to the Lakes by a New *Iter*," *GM* 65 (1795), 564-565.

73. Ann Radcliffe, *A Journey Made in the Summer of 1794 through Holland and the Western Frontier of Germany with a Return down the Rhine* (London: G. G. and J. Robinson, 1795), pp. v-vi; Charles Shephard, "Tour through Wales and the Central Parts of England," *GM* 68 (1798), 304; Edward Burt, *Letters from a Gentleman in the North of Scotland to His Friend in London* (1754), ed. R. Jamieson, 5th ed. (London: Rest Fenner, 1818), I, 10.

74. Paterson, *Another Traveller!*, I, 35-36. Compare Edward Ives's statement: "Should it be objected, that I have treated too minutely of myself and my own concerns; I have only to answer, that the man who writes his own journey, is under a necessity in some degree of making himself the hero of his own tale" (*A Voyage from England to India* [London: E. and C. Dilly, 1773], p. vi).

75. Smith, *Sketch of a Tour*, I, xvi; *CR* 36 (1773), 242. Also see the comment made on William Mavor's *Historical Account of Voyages:* "We object . . . to the form into which he has often thrown the information of the original writers. By a change of the first person to the third, he has diminished the interest, and in some measure altered the character of the narrative" (*CR* 2d ser., 25 [1799], 226).

76. Fielding, *Voyage to Lisbon*, p. 24.

77. The title page of the first edition of Burt's *Letters* (London: S. Birt, 1754) catalogs the following contents: "The Description of a Capital Town in that Northern Country; with An Account of some uncommon Customs of the Inhabitants: likewise An Account of the Highlands, with the *Customs* and *Manners* of the Highlanders. To which is added, A Letter relating to the Military Ways among the Mountains, began in the Year 1726. The Whole interspers'd with *Facts* and *Circumstances* intirely New to the Generality of People in *England,* and little known in the Southern Parts of *Scotland*." Abbé Lambert's *Collection of Curious Observations* (London: For the translator [John Dunn], 1750) likewise describes "Manners, Customs, Usages, different Languages, Government, Mythology, Chronology, Ancient and Modern Geography, Ceremonies, Religion, Mechanics, Astronomy, Medicine, Physics, Natural History, Commerce, Arts, and Sciences, of the several Nations of *Asia, Africa,* and *America*." And William Borlase's *Natural History of Cornwall* (Oxford: For the author, 1758) treats "The Air, Climate, Waters, Rivers, Lakes, Sea and Tides; Of the Stones,

Semimetals, Metals, Tin, and the Manner of Mining, . . . Vegetables, Rare Birds, Fishes, Shells, Reptiles, and Quadrupeds: Of the Inhabitants, Their Manners, Customs. . . . "

78. *CR* 12 (1761), 238; 5 (1758), 32-33; Boswell, *Life of Johnson,* III, 279. Chapter LXXII of Niels Horrebow's book actually reads: "No snakes of any kind are to be met with throughout the whole island" (*The Natural History of Iceland* [London: A. Linde, 1758], p. 91).

79. [John Ward], *MR* 4 (1751), 317; Adam Olearius, *Voyages & Travels of the Ambassadors Sent by Frederick Duke of Holstein,* trans. John Davies (London: T. Dring, 1662), I, 47; Smollett, *Travels,* Letter 22. For an example of a carefully organized natural history, see *England Illustrated* (London: R. & J. Dodsley, 1764). A lengthy comment on its principle of organization appears in *CR* 17 (1764), 25-27.

80. *A New and General Biographical Dictionary* (London: T. Osborne, 1761-1767), IX, 217.

81. Philip Francis, *The Satires of Horace,* 5th ed. (London: A. Millar, 1753), III, 82.

82. [Andrew Swinton or William Thomson], Travels into Norway, Denmark and Russia (London: G. G. J. and J. Robinson, 1792), p. vii; *CR* 2d ser., 26 (1799), 176.

83. *CR* 68 (1789), 175; *Connoisseur,* no. 27; William Paterson, *A Narrative of Four Journeys into the Country of the Hottentots* (London: J. Johnson, 1789), p. vi; Andrew Burnaby, *Burnaby's Travels through North America,* ed. by Rufus Rockwell Wilson (New York: A. Wessels, 1904), p. 23; *MR* 2d ser., 4 (1791), 111; George Cartwright, *Captain Cartwright and His Labrador Journal,* ed. by Charles Wendell Townsend (Boston: D. Estes, 1911), p. 5. For Swift's parody of the use of nautical terms in travel accounts, see *Gulliver's Travels,* Part II, Chapter I.

84. Patrick Campbell, *Travels in the Interior Inhabited Parts of North America,* ed. H. H. Langton (Toronto: Champlain Society, 1937), p. 3; Patrick M'Robert, *A Tour through Parts of the North Provinces of America* (Philadelphia: Historical Society of Pennsylvania, 1935), p. ix; *Letters of Hume,* II, 268-269; Smith, *Sketch of a Tour,* I, xiii. For an attack on this practice, see Henry Swinburne *Travels through Spain* (London: P. Elmsly, 1779), p. iii.

85. *CR* 2d ser., 18 (1796), 136; 1st ser., 48 (1779), 217; 4 (1757), 318-319. For similar comments, see *CR* 2 (1756), 187-188; 4 (1757), 2; 6 (1758), 420; 10 (1760), 341; 15 (1762), 43; 21 (1766), 359; 24 (1767), 157; 25 (1768), 181; 32 (1771), 410; 33 (1772), 304; 36 (1773), 35; 39 (1775), 33; 41 (1776), 355; 42 (1776), 93; 47 (1779), 261, 423; 48 (1779), 280; 66

(1788), 399-400; 2d ser., 18 (1796), 130; 21 (1797), 38-39; *GM* 65 (1795), 569-570; *MR* 3 (1750), 342; 46 (1772), 568; 53 (1775), 211.

86. *The Letters of Anna Seward,* preface by A. Constable (Edinburgh: A. Constable, 1811), II, 294; also see *CR* 68 (1789), 104. For praise of Lady Montagu's style, see *CR* 15 (1762), 426.

87. Johnson's Advertisement for *The World Displayed,* in Allen T. Hazen, *Samuel Johnson's Prefaces & Dedications* (New Haven: Yale University Press, 1937), p. 217.


## II. NARRATIVE CONVENTIONS

1. For Defoe's description of Tunbridge-Wells, see his *Tour through the Whole Island of Great Britain,* intro. G. D. H. Cole and D. C. Browning (London: J. M. Dent, 1962), I, 125-128.

2. John Hawkesworth, *Adventurer* 4; Samuel Ireland, *A Picturesque Tour through Holland, Brabant, and Part of France,* 2d ed. (London: T. & J. Egerton, 1796), I, xii. Also see *CR* 40 (1775), 166.

3. Samuel Johnson, *The Lives of the English Poets,* ed. George Birkbeck Hill (Oxford: Clarendon Press, 1905), III, 299-300; *The Correspondence of Jonathan Swift,* ed. Harold Williams (Oxford: Clarendon Press, 1963-1965), IV, 53; *AR* 7 (1790), 375. James Arbuckle similarly argues for the necessity of augmenting poetic descriptions with narratives of exciting events: "The descriptive part of Poetry, however agreeable to a well-form'd Imagination, raises none of those wonderful Emotions, which are stirred up by a Recital of those Actions, which are attended with Dangers, Distresses and Escapes" (*Hibernicus's Letters,* 2d ed. [London: J. Clark, 1734], I, 424-425). Likewise, in discussing Henry James Pye's *Faringdon Hill; A Poem* (1774), William Woodfall writes that "no talents could render pleasing a long description of a fine prospect, when the several parts of which it is composed are not rendered interesting by some well imagined circumstances and transactions" (*MR* 50 [1774], 484).

4. Tobias Smollett, *Travels through France and Italy,* intro. James Morris (Fontwell, Sussex: Centaur Press, 1969), Letter VIII.

5. Quoted from the title page of the first edition of Smollett's *Travels* (London: R. Baldwin, 1766).

6. Henry Fielding, *The Journal of a Voyage to Lisbon,* ed. Harold E. Pagliaro (New York: Nardon Press, 1963), p. 80. Two editions of *The Journal of a Voyage to Lisbon* appeared soon after Fielding's widow returned to England with the manuscript. In the first edition, published in

February 1755, Fielding's hosts on the Isle of Ryde are named Mr. and Mrs. Humphrys. Though based on Fielding's manuscript, the galley proofs of this edition were revised by John Fielding, the author's half brother, who changed a number of names in order to avoid offending the people his brother had attacked. In November of the same year Lisbon suffered a devastating earthquake. Attempting to capitalize on interest in Lisbon generated by this disaster, Andrew Millar published a second edition (probably in December 1755) in which he relied solely on Fielding's manuscript and ignored the corrections made by his brother. In this edition Fielding's hosts are named Mr. and Mrs. Francis. For a discussion of these two editions, see F. S. Dickson, "The Early Editions of Fielding's *Voyage to Lisbon*," *Library* 3d ser., 8 (1917), 24-35; and J. Paul de Castro, "Henry Fielding's Last Voyage," *Library*, 8 (1917), 145-159.

7. Fielding, *Voyage to Lisbon*, pp. 71-72.

8. J. Paul de Castro prints this letter in "Henry Fielding's Last Voyage," pp. 157-158. Ronald Paulson and Thomas Lockwood, like de Castro, claim that Margaret Collier "possibly" was its author (see *Henry Fielding: The Critical Heritage* [London: Routledge & Kegan Paul, 1969], pp. 391-392). F. Homes Dudden more convincingly identifies its author as Jane Collier (see *Henry Fielding: His Life, Works, and Times* [Oxford: Clarendon Press, 1952], II, 1020-1021).

9. *GM* 25 (1755), 129.

10. John Moore, *A View of Society and Manners in France, Switzerland, and Germany: With Anecdotes Relating to Some Eminent Characters* (London: W. W. Strahan, 1779), I, 4, 8, 10.

11. Ibid., pp. 11-12.

12. *CR* 48 (1779), 209.

13. Quoted from Moore, *A View of Society and Manners in France*, 9th ed. (London: T. Cadell Jun., 1800), I, iii; italics mine.

14. *MR* 46 (1772), 625; 48 (1773), 328; *CR* 15 (1762), 43; Daniel Beeckman, *A Voyage to and from the Island of Borneo* (London: T. Warner, 1718), A5$^r$-A5$^v$. Concerning the truthfulness of Captain Smith's *Travels*, see Philip L. Barbour, "Fact and Fiction in Captain John Smith's *True Travels*," in *Literature as a Mode of Travel*, intro. Warner G. Rice (New York: New York Public Library, 1963), pp. 101-114. Shakespeare alludes to the conventional disbelief of travelers in *The Tempest*, III, iii, 21-27.

15. Boswell, *Life of Johnson*, ed. George Birkbeck Hill and L. F. Powell (Oxford: Clarendon Press, 1934-1950), IV, 320.

16. *CR* 28 (1769), 29.

17. G. Boucher de la Richarderie, *Bibliothèque universelle des voyages* (Paris: Treutte et Würtz, 1808), V, 289-291.

18. *CR* 23 (1767), 456.

19. See Percy G. Adams, *Travelers and Travel Liars: 1660-1800* (Berkeley and Los Angeles: University of California Press, 1962), Chap. II.

20. See Thomas Seccombe's Introduction to *The Surprising Adventures of Baron Munchausen* (London: Lawrence, 1895), pp. xxxi-xxxii. For a thorough discussion of Bruce's reception in England, see Adams, *Travelers*, pp. 210-222.

21. *GM* 59 (1789), 544.

22. Countess Danois [Marie Catherine Jumelle de Berneville, comtesse d'Aulnoy], *The Lady's Travels into Spain; Or, a Genuine Relation of the Religion, Laws, Commerce, Customs, and Manners of that Country*, new ed. (London: T. Davies, 1774), I, xi.

23. See, for instance, *AR* 10 (1791), 170.

24. Henry Swinburne, *Travels through Spain* (London: P. Elmsly, 1779), p. v; Johannes Aegidius van Egmond and Johannes Heyman, *Travels through Part of Europe, Asia Minor, the Islands of the Archipelago* (London: L. Davis, 1759), I, v-vi.

25. *CR* 31 (1771), 238-239; concerning the fictional nature of J. G. Dubois-Fontanelle's *Shipwreck and Adventures of Mons. Pierre Viaud*, see James Stanier Clarke, *Naufragia; Or, Historical Memoirs of Shipwrecks and of the Providential Deliverance of Vessels* (London: J. Mawman, 1805-1806), II, viii.

26. *MR* 45 (1771), 330. For similar comments, see *CR* 30 (1770), 436; 33 (1772), 456; 35 (1773), 61; *MR* 57 (1777), 243; *LM* 45 (1776), 548.

27. *MR* 47 (1772), 38, 252; *CR* 33 (1772), 360. For a discussion of the authenticity of *A Journal of a Voyage . . . in His Majesty's Ship Endeavour*, see Edward Godfrey Cox, *A Reference Guide to the Literature of Travel*, (Seattle: University of Washington Press, 1935-1949), I, 54-55. Concerning Marshall's *Travels*, see *Annual Register . . . for the Year 1772*, "Account of Books"; John Pinkerton, *The Literary Correspondence of John Pinkerton* (London: H. Colburn, 1830), II, 231-232, 324.

28. William Combe, *The Tour of Doctor Syntax in Search of the Picturesque*, new ed. (London: Methuen, 1903), p. 198.

29. Tobias Smollett, *The Expeditions of Humphry Clinker,* Jery Melford to Watkin Phillips, London, June 10; *CR* 21 (1766), 280-281. For other descriptions of this kind of travel writer, see Richard Savage, *An Author To Be Lett* (1729), ed. James Sutherland (Los Angeles: William Andrews Clark Memorial Library, 1960), pp. 3-4; *CR* 12 (1761), 439; *UM* 103 (1798), 338; *Travels of Carl Philipp Moritz in England in 1782*, intro. P. E. Matheson (London: H. Milford, 1926), p. 4; *GM* 18 (1748), 563.

30. *AR* 3 (1789), 57.

31. *CR* 28 (1769), 331. Also see *CR* 34 (1772), 400.

32. *MR* 42 (1770), 329. Field-Lane extended from Holborn to Clerken-well in an extremely poor area of London (see William J. Pinks, *The History of Clerkenwell,* ed. Edward J. Wood, 2d ed. [London: C. Herbert, 1881], pp. 353, 377, 382, 387).

33. Archibald Campbell, *The Sale of Authors: A Dialogue in Imitation of Lucian's Sale of Philosophers* (London: n.p., 1767), p. 187.

34. *A Collection of Voyages and Travels,* ed. Awnsham and John Churchill, 3d ed. (London: H. Lintot, 1744-1746), VI, bi$^r$.

35. *CR* 2d ser., 22 (1798), 491-492.

36. Adams, *Travelers,* p. 17; also see p. 235.

37. See Jean Baptiste du Halde, *Description géographique, historique . . . de l'empire de la Chine et de la Tartarie chinoise* (Paris: P. G. Lemer-cier, 1735), pp. ii-iii.

38. Adams, *Travelers,* p. 89.

39. *CR* 2d ser., 24 (1798), 453.

40. See, for instance, Samuel Stanhope Smith, *An Essay on the Causes of the Variety of Complexion and Figure in the Human Species* (1787), ed. Winthrop D. Jordan (Cambridge, Mass.: Belknap Press of the Harvard University Press, 1965), passim.

41. See, for instance, William Edward Mead, *The Grand Tour in the Eighteenth Century* (Boston: Houghton Mifflin, 1914), pp. 273-283.

42. *CR* 2d ser., 27 (1799), 286, 289; ibid., 206, 207.

43. *MR* 41 (1769), 44-45.

44. *CR* 24 (1767), 177; the *CR* here hints at a false etymology, *rhodo-montade,* usually spelled *rodomontade,* coming not from *Rhodes* but from *Rodomonte* (literally "roll-mountain" in Italian), the name of the boastful Saracen leader in Matteo Maria Boiardo's *Orlando Innamorato* (1483) and Ludovico Ariosto's *Orlando Furioso* (1516).

45. *MR* 39 (1768), 111; also see *CR* 39 (1775), 217-218.

46. For Laurence Sterne's use of these terms, see *A Sentimental Journey through France and Italy,* ed. G. D. Stout (Berkeley and Los Angeles: University of California Press, 1967), p. 81.

47. Jérôme Richard, *Description historique et critique de l'Italie* (Dijon: F. des Ventes, 1766), I, i-ii.

48. Samuel Johnson, *Idler* 97; also see *The Letters of Samuel Johnson,* ed. R. W. Chapman (Oxford: Clarendon Press, 1952), I, 341. Oliver Gold-smith likewise censures whirlwind travelers in *The Citizen of the World,* Letter 122, and Samuel Foote points out this typical characteristic by giv-ing the name Peter Hasty to the "Voyage-writer" mentioned in Act I, scene

i. of *The Author* (1757). Also see *The Bee* for 27 March 1793; *Travels of Moritz*, p. 11.

49. Laurence Sterne, *The Life and Opinions of Tristram Shandy, Gentleman*, ed. James Aikin Work (New York: Odyssey Press, 1940), p. 502; Samuel Paterson, *Another Traveller! or Cursory Remarks and Tritical Observations Made upon a Journey through Part of the Netherlands in the Latter End of the Year 1766* (London: J. Johnson, 1767-1769), I, 121-122, 289.

50. Thomas Cogan, *The Rhine; Or, a Journey from Utrecht to Frankfort* (1794), cited in Geoffrey Trease, *The Grand Tour* (New York: Heinemann, 1967), p. 5. Also see *AR* 8 (1790), 155.

51. Arthur Young, *Travels in France during the Years 1787, 1788 & 1789*, ed. Constantia Maxwell (Cambridge: Cambridge University Press, 1929), p. liv.

52. *PR* 2 (1768), 64; *MR* 38 (1768), 222; 42 (1770), 269.

53. *CR* 34 (1772), 99-100, 102; [Jebez Hirons], *MR* 47 (1772), 165. For similar comments about other travel books, see *CR* 33 (1772), 14; 43 (1777), 432, 438; 68 (1789), 44; 2d ser., 22 (1798), 372, 378.

54. Swinburne, *Travels through Spain*, p. iv. For similar comments, see [Andrew Swinton or William Thomson], *Travels into Norway, Denmark and Russia* (London: G. G. J. and J. Robinson, 1792), p. v.

55. Hester Lynch Thrale Piozzi, *Observations and Reflections Made in the Course of a Journey through France, Italy, and Germany*, ed. Herbert Barrows (Ann Arbor: University of Michigan Press, 1967), pp. 389, 390.

56. *MR* 43 (1770), 223; Samuel Pratt, *Travels for the Heart* (London: J. Wallis, 1777), I, xxxvi.

57. *Remarks and Collections of Thomas Hearne*, ed. C. E. Doble (Oxford: Clarendon Press, 1885-1921), I, 168.

58. Macrobius, *The Saturnalia*, trans. Percival Vaughan Davies (New York: Columbia University Press, 1969), p. 349; italics mine.

59. Paterson, *Another Traveller!*, I, 195; Andrew Burnaby, *Travels through North America*, ed. Rufus Rockwell Wilson (New York: A. Wessels, 1904), p. 22; *MR* 55 (1776), 401-402.

60. Robert Gray, *Letters during the Course of a Tour through Germany, Switzerland and Italy* (London: F. and C. Rivington, 1794), p. iii; for similar introductory statements, see Anna Riggs Miller, *Letters from Italy* (London: E. and C. Dilly, 1776), I, vi-vii; Samuel Ireland, *A Picturesque Tour through Holland*, I, xii; John Hassell, *Tour of the Isle of Wight* (London: T. Hookham, 1790), I, vii; Samuel Holmes, *Journal... during His Attendance... on Lord Macartney's Embassy to China and Tartary*

(London: W. Bulmer, 1798), advertisement; William Paterson, *A Narrative of Four Journeys into the Country of the Hottentots* (London: J. Johnson, 1789), p. vi. Also note the title of Sacheverell Stevens's *Miscellaneous Remarks Made on the Spot, in a Late Seven Years' Tour through France, Germany and Holland* (1756).

61. *MR* 45 (1771), 212; for similar comments, see *CR* 31 (1771), 121; 68 (1789), 421 (misnumbered 491); *AR* 9 (1791), 409. For an attack on a travel book not written "on the spot," see *CR* 68 (1789), 113.

62. Leopold Berchtold, *An Essay to Direct and Extend the Inquiries of Patriotic Travellers* (London: For the author, 1789), I, 43. For a similar comment, see John Coakley Lettsom, *The Naturalist's and Traveller's Companion*, 3d ed. (London: C. Dilly, 1799), p. xvi.

63. See, for example, *Tour*, I, 12.

64. Samuel Johnson, *A Journey to the Western Islands of Scotland*, ed. Mary Lascelles (New Haven: Yale University Press, 1971), pp. 146-147; compare Jacob Spon's *Voyage d'Italie* (1678-1680) with George Wheler's *Journey into Greece* (1682).

65. See *Letters of Samuel Johnson*, ed. Chapman, I, 370.

66. See, for example, *British Critic* 2 (1793), 430-431.

67. *MR* 28 (1763), 215. Also see "Directions for Sea-men, bound for far Voyages," in *The Philosophical Transactions of the Royal Society*, I (1666), 140-143; Ray W. Frantz, *The English Traveller and the Movement of Ideas, 1660-1732* (Lincoln: University of Nebraska Press, 1967), Chap. I; Samuel Stanhope Smith, *An Essay on the Causes of the Variety of Complexion and Figure in the Human Species*, p. 129n.

68. See Scott B. Rice, "The Significance of Smollett's Weather Register," *N&Q* 215 (1970), 94-95. Similar meteorological accounts appear in Alexander Drummond's *Travels through Different Cities of Germany, Italy, Greece and Several Parts of Asia;* Edward Ives's *Voyage from England to India* (1773); J. H.'s "Meteorologist's Tour from Walton to London," *GM* 63 (1793), 619-621, 720-721; Andrew Burnaby's *Travels through the Middle Settlements in North America;* and John White's *Journal of a Voyage to New South Wales* (1790). Along similar lines, Joseph Robson includes a journal of winds and tides at the end of his *Account of Six Years Residence in Hudson's-Bay* (1752).

69. William Forbes, *An Account of the Life and Writings of James Beattie, LL.D.* (Edinburgh: A. Constable, 1806), I, 392.

70. Francis R. Hart, "Johnson as Philosophic Traveler: The Perfecting of an Idea," *ELH* 36 (1969), 691.

71. Boswell, *An Account of Corsica, the Journal of a Tour to that Island, and Memoirs of Pascal Paoli,* 3d ed. (London: E. and C. Dilly, 1769), p. 317; *AR* 18 (1794), 417.

72. *LC* 34 (1773), 244; Michel Adanson, *A Voyage to Senegal* (London: J. Nourse, 1759), p. vii; Berchtold, *Essay,* I, 85; François Marie Arouet de Voltaire, *An Essay upon the Civil Wars* (London: S. Jallasson, 1727), Advertisement. Voltaire's *Letters concerning the English Nation* (English 1733; French 1734), lacking as it does a narrative framework, is not properly speaking a travel account; yet its philosophical spirit, if not its form, appears to have fostered many imitations.

73. Boswell, *Life of Johnson,* III, 236; Staffa [pseud.], "Anecdote of the Last Hebridean Traveller," *St. James's Chronicle,* no. 2191 (28 Feb.-2 March 1775). Also see V. S. Pritchett, "The Unhappy Traveller," in *Books in General* (New York: Harcourt Brace, n.d.), pp. 88-93.

74. *AR* 8 (1790), 160.

75. John Hill, *Hypochondriasis: A Practical Treatise* (1766), intro. G. S. Rousseau (Los Angeles: William Andrews Clark Memorial Library, 1969), pp. 6-7, 8. Also see Cecil A. Moore, "The English Malady," in *Backgrounds of English Literature, 1700-1760* (Minneapolis: University of Minnesota Press, 1953), pp. 179-235.

76. Lord Gardenstone, *Travelling Memorandums* (Edinburgh: Bell & Bradfute, 1791), I, 43-44; also see p. 5.

77. Giuseppe Baretti, *An Account of the Manners and Customs of Italy,* 2d ed. (London: T. Davies, 1769), II, 320, 324.

78. *AR* 7 (1790), 393.

79. William Gilpin, "On Picturesque Travel," in *Three Essays* (London: R. Blamire, 1792), pp. 42, 57.

80. William Gilpin, *Observations Relative Chiefly to Picturesque Beauty, Made in the year 1776, on Several Parts of Great Britain; Particularly the High-Lands of Scotland* (London: R. Blamire, 1789), II, 23, 193; Ireland, *Picturesque Tour through Holland,* II, 197.

81. Vicesimus Knox, *Essays, Moral and Literary,* 5th ed. (London: C. Dilly, 1784), I, 117; John Ferrar, *A Tour from Dublin to London* (Dublin: n.p., 1796), p. iv [bound with Ferrar, *A View of Ancient and Modern Dublin* (Dublin: n.p., 1796)]. Concerning Knox's not always favorable opinion of Sterne, see Alan B. Howes, *Yorick and the Critics: Sterne's Reputation in England, 1760-1868* (New Haven: Yale University Press, 1958), pp. 74-76.

82. William Roberts, *Looker-on* 73. The catalog of books in the library

of Thomas Stanley lists travel accounts in a section titled "Voyages, Travels, and Picturesque Tours" (*Bibliotheca Stanleiana* [London: W. Bulmer, 1813]).

83. William Combe, *Pic Nic* 10 (12 March 1803), printed in *The Pic Nic* (London: J. F. Hughes, 1803), II, 132. Concerning the relative popularities of *Sentimental Journey* and *Tristram Shandy,* see Howes, *Yorick and the Critics,* pp. 40, 65, 67-68.

84. J. M. S. Tompkins, *The Popular Novel in England: 1770-1800* (1932; rpt. London: Methuen, 1961), p. 52.

85. "Recent Travels," *Fraser's Magazine* 46 (1852), 245; "Travels and Travellers," *Dublin University Magazine* 22 (1843), 154. Also see "Unpublished Journals of Travel," *Fraser's Magazine* 50 (1854), 80-81.

86. *Memoirs of the Extraordinary Life, Works, and Discoveries of Martinus Scriblerus,* ed. Charles Kerby-Miller (New York: Russell & Russell, 1950), p. 101; Robert Brown, "Twelve Months of Travel," *Fortnightly Review* 40 (1883), 380. Also see "Recent Travellers," *Fraser's Magazine* 42 (1850), 44.

87. See *North American Review* 79 (1854), 98.

88. *British Critic* 4 (1794), 391.


## III. DESCRIPTIVE CONVENTIONS

1. Hester Lynch Thrale Piozzi, *Observations and Reflections Made in the Course of a Journey through France, Italy, and Germany,* ed. Herbert Barrows (Ann Arbor: University of Michigan Press, 1967), pp. 46, 48, 85, 86; Henry Fielding, *The Journal of a Voyage to Lisbon,* ed. Harold E. Pagliaro (New York: Nardon Press, 1963), pp. 106-108; William Gilpin, *Observations Relative Chiefly to Picturesque Beauty, Made in the Year 1776, on Several Parts of Great Britain; Particularly the High-Lands of Scotland* (London: R. Blamire, 1789), II, 33-35.

2. Edward Young, *Night Thoughts,* "Night I," lines 47-48.

3. See James Thomson's "Argument to Winter" in his *Poetical Works,* ed. J. Logie Robertson (London: Oxford University Press, 1908), p. 184.

4. See Ralph Cohen, *The Art of Discrimination* (Berkeley and Los Angeles: University of California Press, 1964), p. 108, and Robert Heron's "Critical Essay on the Season," in *The Seasons* (Perth: R. Morison, 1793), p. 5.

5. *CR* 3 (1757), 516; Austin Dobson, "Hanway's Travels," in *Eighteenth Century Vignettes: First Series* (London: H. Milford, 1923), p. 79.

6. *CR* 3 (1757), 516; 4 (1757), 1; *MR* 49 (1773), 515. For further distinctions between observations and reflections, see *CR* 41 (1776), 235; *GM* 62 (1792), 930. Occasionally *description* or *object* appears in place of *observation,* and *sentiment* or *opinion* appears in place of *reflection* (see *CR* 44 [1777], 48; 2d ser., 18 [1796], 386; Henry Skrine, *Three Successive Tours in the North of England and Great Parts of Scotland* [London: W. Bulmer, 1795], p. 5). Mrs. Piozzi occasionally gets *observation* and *reflection* confused (see, for instance, *Observations and Reflections,* pp. 87, 332).

7. Johann Georg Keyssler, *Travels through Germany, Bohemia, Hungary, Switzerland, Italy, and Lorrain,* 3d ed. (London: G. Keith, 1760), Letter XXVIII; also see Letters VI and IX.

8. *Miscellaneous Works of Edward Gibbon,* ed. John Lord Sheffield (London: A. Strahan, 1796), II, 302. For a discussion of the revisions and translations of Keyssler's *Neueste Reise* (1740), see *Biographie universelle ancienne et moderne,* nouvelle ed. (Paris: Chez Madame C. Desplaces, 1854-[1865]), XXI, 562.

9. Edward Godfrey Cox, *A Reference Guide to the Literature of Travel* (Seattle: University of Washington Press, 1935-1949), I, 116. Concerning the editions, translations, and revisions of Misson's *Voyage,* see Cox, *Reference Guide.*

10. Quoted from the title page of *The Travels of Mr. Maximilien Misson* as it appears in John Harris's *Navigantium atque itinerantium bibliotheca* (1744-1748), and from the title page of the first edition of Defoe's *Tour thro' the Whole Island of Great Britain* (London: G. Strahan, 1724-1727).

11. *CR* 46 (1778), 452; concerning the revisions of Defoe's *Tour,* see Godfrey Davies, "Daniel Defoe's *A Tour thro' the Whole Island of Great Britain,*" *MP* 48 (1950), 21-36.

12. See George Martyn Barringer, "Defoe's *A Tour thro' the Whole Island of Great Britain,*" *Thoth* 9 (1968), 3-13; Pat Rogers, "Literary Art in Defoe's *Tour:* The Rhetoric of Growth and Decay," *Eighteenth-Century Studies* 6 (1972-1973), 153-185.

13. Samuel Paterson, *Another Traveller! or Cursory Remarks and Tritical Observations Made upon a Journey through Part of the Netherlands in the Latter End of the Year 1766* (London: J. Johnson, 1767-1769), I, 410, 458-459.

14. Leopold Berchtold, *An Essay to Direct and Extend the Inquiries of Patriotic Travellers* (London: For the author, 1789), I, 19-20, passim. Berchtold also suggests that the traveler ask questions about colonies, inland navigation, navigation upon the sea, sea ports, fishery in general, herring fishery, whale fishery, coral fishery, construction of merchantmen,

laws and administration of civil justice, laws and administration of criminal justice, police, charitable establishments, education, origin, manners, and customs of the nation, women, religion and clergy, nobility, government, taxes and imposts, finances, land forces, navy, construction of men of war, and sovereigns.

15. *AR* 5 (1789), 313-318; *CR* 68 (1789), 330-331; *GM* 59 (1789), 1015-1017; *MR* 81 (1789), 351-352.

16. Robert Essex, Philip Sidney, William Davison, *Profitable Instructions* (London: B. Fisher, 1633), pp. 2-7.

17. Bishop Tucker, *Instructions for Travellers* ([London?]: n.p., 1757), pp. 10, 58-61. More complex than Tucker's *Instructions* is Dr. Lettsom's *Naturalist's and Traveller's Companion* (1772; enlarged 1774), which after giving precise instructions concerning how to capture insects, bring live plants back to England and the like, suggests the following subjects to be inquired into by the English traveler: (1) "Learning, Antiquities, religious Rites, polite Arts, &c.," (2) "Commerce, Manufacture, Arts, Trade, &c.," (3) "Meterological Observations, Food, Way of Living, Animal OEconomy in general, &c.," (4) "Zoology," (5) "Botany," and (6) "Mineralogy." Under these topics, Lettsom moreover lists subtopics, sometimes as many as twenty-three, which direct the traveler's attention to particular problems.

18. Tobias Smollett, *Travels through France and Italy,* intro. James Morris (Fontwell, Sussex: Centaur Press, 1969), Letter XXVIII; *Literary Magazine* 1 (1756), 240; Johann Winckelmann, *Geschichte der Kunst des Altertums* (1764; Vienna: Phaidon, 1934), p. 12. Arthur Sherbo suggests that Dr. Johnson wrote the review of Keyssler's *Travels* for the *Literary Magazine* ("A Possible Addition to the Johnson Canon," *Review of English Studies,* new ser., 6 [1955], 70-71).

19. Fielding, *Voyage to Lisbon,* p. 24; Joseph Palmer, *A Four Months Tour through France* (Dublin: S. Price, 1776), I, 7; William Thomson, *Travels in Europe, Asia, and Africa* (London: J. Murray, 1782), p. iv. The *Monthly Review* similarly defines novelty as "that curiosity which prompts us to read books of travels with greater avidity than any others" (*MR* 48 [1772], 418).

20. *CR* 1 (1756), 309. Thomas Francklin seems to have written this review (see Derek Roper, "Smollett's 'Four Gentlemen': The First Contributors to the *Critical Review,*" *Review of English Studies,* new ser., 10 [1959], 38-44).

21. *CR* 21 (1766), 359-360; 39 (1775), 33; 68 (1789), 107. The *Critical Review* here refers to John Moore's *View of Society and Manners in Italy* (1781).

22. *CR* 2d ser., 18 (1796), 386. For similar comments, see *CR* 31 (1771), 119; 37 (1774), 10; 2d ser., 26 (1799), 167, 269; *MR* 45 (1771), 209.

23. *CR* 47 (1779), 376.

24. Boswell, *Life of Johnson,* ed. George Birkbeck Hill and L. F. Powell (Oxford: Clarendon Press, 1934-1950), III, 36; for a discussion of theories concerning the educational value of the grand tour, see George B. Parks, "Travel as Education," in *The Seventeenth Century, by Richard Foster Jones, and Other Writings in His Honor* (Stanford: Stanford University Press, 1951), pp. 264-290; George C. Brauer, Jr., *The Education of a Gnelteman* (New York: Bookman Associates, 1959), pp. 156-194.

25. Piozzi, *Observations and Reflections,* p. 247; also see John Owen, *Travels into Different Parts of Europe* (London: T. Cadell, Jun., 1796), I, iv-v; *CR* 2d ser., 18 (1796), 416.

26. Giuseppe Baretti, *A Journey from London to Genoa* (London: T. Davies, 1770), I, v [fonts reversed]; Boswell, *Life of Johnson,* I, 365; *CR* 30 (1770), 197; Richard Twiss, *Travels through Portugal and Spain* (London: For the author, 1775), p. ii. Other imitations of Baretti's *Journey* during the 1770s include Joseph Marshall, *Travels through France and Spain* (1776); John Blankett, *Letters from Portugal* (1777); Francis Carter, *A Journey from Gibraltar to Malaga* (1777); William Dalrymple, *Travels through Spain and Portugal* (1777); Philip Thicknesse, *A Year's Journey through France, and Part of Spain* (1777); Henry Swinburne, *Travels through Spain* (1779). For a complete list, see Raymond Foulché-Delbosc, "Bibliographie des voyages en Espagne et en Portugal," *Revue hispanique* 3 (1896), 1-349. The standard travel description of Spain before Baretti's *Journey* was Madam D'Aulnoy's *Relation du voyage d'Espagne* (1691), immediately translated as *The Ingenious and Diverting Letters of the Lady —— Travels into Spain* and reprinted in English, sometimes under different titles, at least twelve times before 1800. Countess D'Aulnoy, as she liked to be called, unfortunately never visited the country she described (see Raymond Foulché-Delbosc, "Introduction," *Travels into Spain* [New York: R. M. McBride, 1930], pp. xxviii-lxxiii). Edward Clarke's *Letters concerning the Spanish Nation,* appearing some seven years before Baretti's *Journey,* is not actually a travel account (see *CR* 15 [1763], 295-296).

27. *CR* 25 (1768), 185; *MR* 53 (1775), 11.

28. Nathaniel Wraxall, *A Tour round the Baltic through the Northern Countries of Europe,* 4th ed. (London: T. Cadell, 1807), p. 2; Wraxall, *A Tour through the Western, Southern, and Interior Provinces of France,* 3d ed. (London: J. Mawman, 1807), pp. 279-280.

29. George Otto Trevelyan, *The Early History of Charles James Fox* (London: Longmans, 1880), p. 153. Prior to Boswell's *Account,* the only

book-length descriptions of the island were Jean François Goury de Champgrand's *Histoire de l'isle de Corse* (1749) and Louis Armand Jaussin's *Mémoires historiques, militaires et politiques* (1758-1759).

30. *CR* 16 (1763), 75; 23 (1767), 309. Also see James L. Clifford, "Doctor Thomas Campbell, 1733-1795," in *Dr. Campbell's Diary of a Visit to England in 1775,* ed. James L. Clifford (Cambridge: Cambridge University Press, 1947), p. 6.

31. Jack Simmons, *Journeys in England: An Anthology* (London: Odhams Press, 1951), p. 18. For a discussion of travel in England prior to the eighteenth century, see Virginia A. LaMar, *Travel and Roads in England,* Folger Booklets on Tudor and Stuart Civilization (Washington: Folger Shakespeare Library, 1960).

32. Such travels, however, never achieved the social status enjoyed by the grand tour. The *Gentleman's Magazine,* for instance, always mentions in its obituary notices that the deceased had made the grand tour, but never that he had traveled about his own country (see Esther Moir, *The Discovery of Britain: The English Tourists* [London: Routledge & Kegan Paul, 1964], p. xiii). A tour through Great Britain, at least to Bishop Tucker, gradually began to serve as one of the prerequisites for going abroad on the grand tour (see Tucker, *Instructions,* p. 4).

33. See *Pamela,* intro. M. Kinkead-Weekes (London: J. M. Dent, 1962), II, 230, 341, 380-381, 419.

34. *CR* 2d ser., 18 (1796), 129.

35. *Monthly Magazine* (1778), cited in Cox, *Reference Guide,* III, 24. For a description of the discovery of the Lake District, see William Gershom Collingwood, *Lake District History,* new ed. (Kendal: T. Wilson, 1928), pp. 155-171.

36. *LM* 47 (1778), 179. Travel in Great Britain was also cheaper and less morally dangerous than travel on the Continent: "Were our young noblemen and gentlemen to travel more in their own than in foreign countries, they would, at least, be as highly entertained, and squander much less of their fortunes and their innocence than they commonly do.... Would not a tour round the islands of Great Britain and Ireland furnish a Briton with more useful, proper and entertaining knowledge, than what is called *the grand tour of Europe?* which, for one person that it hath improved, hath been the destruction of thousands!" ([James Robertson], *MR* 37 [1767], 281-282).

37. Robert Bracey, *Eighteenth Century Studies and Other Papers* (Oxford: B. Blackwell, 1925), p. 30.

38. Edward Burt, *Letters from a Gentleman* (London: S. Birt, 1754), title page.

39. See, for example, Arthur Young, *Travels in France during the Years 1787, 1788 & 1789* (1792); Edward Wright, *Some Observations Made in Travelling through France, Italy, &c.* (1730); Charles Burney, *The Present State of Music in France and Italy; or, The Journal of a Tour through Those Countries* (1771); Thomas Pennant, *A Tour in Scotland* (1771); Johann Jakob Ferber, *Travels through Italy* (1776); Andrew Ducarel, *A Tour through Normandy* (1754); John Howard, *The State of Prisons in England* (1777); Helen Maria Williams, *Letters Written in France* (1790); John Dillon, *Letters from an English Traveller in Spain* (1781).

40. *AR* 7 (1790), 375. Concerning Robert Heron, who was neither "an agricultural, a commercial, a virtuoso, nor an antiquarian traveller," see Heron, *Observations Made in a Journey through the Western Counties of Scotland,* cited in *CR* 2d ser., 18 (1796), 380.

41. Edward Topham, *Letters from Edinburgh* (London: J. Dodsley, 1776), p. 368.

42. Johnson, *Rasselas,* Chap. XXX.

43. *CR* 8 (1759), 486-487; translation of Horace's Epistle I. 2. 19-20 by H. Rushton Fairclough (*Satires, Epistles and Ars poetica,* Loeb Classical Library [Cambridge, Mass.: Harvard University Press, 1937], pp. 263, 265). Concerning Ulysses as a model for travelers, see James Howell, *Instructions for Forreine Travell* (1642), ed. E. Arber (Westminster: A. Constable, 1903), p. 13; *The Miscellaneous Works of Sir Philip Sidney, Knt.,* ed. William Gray (Oxford: D. A. Talboys, 1829), pp. 278-283.

44. Abraham Anquetil-Duperron, *Dignité du commerce* (1789), cited in *AR* 5 (1798), 129; Wraxall, *Tour round the Baltic,* p. 1. Also see *Spectator* 474.

45. *CR* 25 (1768), 187-188; *Letters of Samuel Johnson,* ed. R. W. Chapman (Oxford: Clarendon Press, 1952), I, 259; Fielding, *Voyage to Lisbon,* p. 26. H. Rushton Fairclough translates this passage from Horace's *Ars poetica* 142; Ulysses "saw the wide world, its ways and cities all" (*Satires,* p. 463). *Ars poetica* 142 is simply a Latin translation of *Odyssey* 1.2. John Owen cites yet another classical precedent to justify his principle of selection in *Travels into Different Parts of Europe* (1796). On his title page, he quotes Virgil's *Georgics* 4.5: "Mores, et Studia, et Populos," translated by H. Rushton Fairclough as "a whole nation's character and tastes and tribes" (*Eclogues, Georgics, and Aeneid, Books I-VI,* Loeb Classical Library, rev. ed. [Cambridge, Mass.: Harvard University Press, 1950], p. 197).

46. *AR* 5 (1789), 463; *CR* 39 (1775), 44; *MR* 52 (1775), 57.

47. Christopher Hussey, *The Picturesque: Studies in a Point of View* (London: G. P. Putnam's Sons, 1927), p. 100; Cox, *Reference Guide,* III,

21; George B. Parks, "The Turn to the Romantic in the Travel Literature of the Eighteenth Century," *MLQ* 25 (1964), 23, 24, 32.

48. [Goldsmith], *CR* 7 (1759), 505; 32 (1771), 143-144; also see [Gilbert Stuart], *MR* 42 (1770), 510.

49. Berchtold, *Essay*, I, 20.

50. *CR* 10 (1760), 224.

51. [Ralph Griffiths], *MR* 39 (1768), 434-435; here Griffiths paraphrases *Paradise Lost* 3, 489-495. For similar comments, see *CR* 21 (1766), 409; 38 (1774), 400; *MR* 38 (1768), 222-223; 42 (1770), 268; 53 (1775), 17; Paterson, *Another Traveller!*, I, 120-121, 451-452.

52. Paterson, *Another Traveller!*, I, 227; also see p. 261.

53. Ibid., I, 222; Vicesimus Knox, *Essays, Moral and Literary*, 5th ed. (London: C. Dilly, 1784), I, 116. For similar comments, see *CR* 48 (1779), 250; 2d ser., 24 (1798), 409; [Thomas James Mathias], *The Pursuits of Literature*, 14th ed. (London: T. Becket, 1808), p. 71.

54. Paterson, *Another Traveller!*, I, 220-221. For similar comments, see *The Correspondence of Jonathan Swift*, ed. Harold Williams (Oxford: Clarendon Press, 1963-1965), II, 399; William Combe, *The Tour of Dr. Syntax in Search of the Picturesque*, new ed. (London: Methuen, 1903), p. 54; *The Travellers* (London: P. Shatwell, 1778), p. 18; [Ralph Griffiths], *MR* 3 (1750), 343.

55. See *CR* 24 (1767), 172; 39 (1775), 358; 40 (1775), 290.

56. Paterson, *Another Traveller!*, I, 221; *CR* 27 (1769), 53; *Another Traveller!*, I, 223; Goldsmith, *Citizen of the World*, Letter 122.

57. Edward Topham, *Letters from Edinburgh*, pp. vi-vii; [Harry Peckham], *The Tour of Holland, Dutch Brabant, the Austrian Netherlands, and Part of France* (1772), quoted in *CR* 34 (1772), 131.

58. William Forbes, *An Account of the Life and Writings of James Beattie, LL.D.* (Edinburgh: A. Constable, 1806), I, 284; *AR* 8 (1790), 155. For similar comments, see [William Melmoth], *Letters on Several Subjects. By the Late Sir James Fitzosborne* (London: R. Dodsley, 1748-1749), I, 4; *AR* 5 (1789), 463; *GM* 12 (1742), 320; *UM* 103 (1798), 340; Pierre Poivre, *Travels of a Philosopher* (Dublin: P. and W. Wilson, 1770), p. 3.

59. *The Anecdotes and Egotisms of Henry Mackenzie: 1745-1831*, ed. Harold William Thompson (Oxford: H. Milford, 1927), p. 219; *The Early Diary of Frances Burney: 1768-1778*, ed. Annie Raine Ellis (London: G. Bell, 1913), I, 24 [fonts reversed].

60. *UM* 103 (1798), 340; Francis Osborne, *Advice to a Son*, intro. Edward Abbott Parry, new ed. (London: D. Nutt, 1896), p. 62; James Puckle, *The Club* (1711; rpt. ed., [London]: J. Johnson, 1817), p. 45

61. Forbes, *Account of James Beattie*, I, 392.

62. Skrine, *Three Successive Tours*, p. 5; Thomson, *The Seasons*, "Spring," lines 468-477; Ann Radcliffe, *A Journey Made in the Summer of 1794 through Holland and the Western Frontier of Germany with a Return down the Rhine* (London: G. G. and J. Robinson, 1795), p. 419; Piozzi, *Observations and Reflections*, p. 15; Wraxall, *Cursory Remarks*, cited in *CR* 40 (1775), 33.

63. Patrick Brydone, *A Tour through Sicily and Malta*, 3d ed. (London: W. Strahan, 1774), I, 106-108, 202-204.

64. Edmund Burke, *A Philosophical Enquiry into the Origin of Our Ideas of the Sublime and Beautiful* (1757), ed. James T. Boulton (London: Routledge & Kegan Paul, 1958), p. 167; Gotthold Ephraim Lessing, *Laocoon: An Essay on the Limits of Painting and Poetry* (1766), trans. Edward Allen McCormick (Indianapolis: Bobbs-Merrill, 1962), Chap. XVI.

65. *MR* 49 (1773), 120-121.

66. *LM* 42 (1773), 195; also see *CR* 35 (1773), 301; Boswell, *Life of Johnson*, II, 346; Burney, *Early Diary*, ed. Ellis, I, 215; Paul Kaufman, *Borrowings from the Bristol Library: 1773-1784* (Charlottesville: Bibliographical Society of the University of Virginia, 1960), pp. 29, 122; Paul Fussell, "Patrick Brydone: The Eighteenth-Century Traveler as Representative Man," in *Literature as a Mode of Travel,* intro. Warner G. Rice (New York: New York Public Library, 1963), pp. 53-67.

67. J. M. S. Tompkins, *The Popular Novel in England: 1770-1800* (London: Methuen, 1961), p. 255; also see Raymond D. Havens, "Ann Radcliffe's Nature Descriptions," *MLN* 66 (1951), 251-255.

68. *CR* 2d ser., 14 (1795), 241-242; *MR* 2d ser., 18 (1795), 245, where Radcliffe's *Journey*, p. 366 is cited.

69. *CR* 2d ser., 14 (1795), 242.

70. *DNB* VII, 1263; William Gilpin, *Three Essays* (London: R. Blamire, 1792), pp. 41-58.

71. John Nichols, *Literary Anecdotes* (London: For the author, 1812-1816), VIII, 657; *CR* 57 (1783), 53; Mathias, *Pursuits of Literature*, p. 345.

72. *Diary and Letters of Madame D'Arblay: 1778-1840,* ed. Charlotte Barrett and Austin Dobson (London: Macmillan, 1904-1905), II, 397; *Annual Register...for the Year 1789,* "Account of Books." For similar critical comments, see *CR* 64 (1786), 93-100; 68 (1789), 518-523; 2d ser., 24 (1798), 408-414; *MR* 69 (1783), 361-367; 78 (1788), 314-319.

73. Samuel Ireland, *A Picturesque Tour through Holland, Brabant, and Part of France,* 2d ed. (London: T. & J. Egerton, 1769), I, 2-3; *MR* 2d ser., 5 (1791), 94.

74. *GM* 61 (1791), 49; italics are supplied by the reviewer. For the pas-

sage he criticizes, see John Hassell, *Tour of the Isle of Wight* (London: T. Hookham, 1790), I, 103.

75. *GM* 61 (1791), 50.

76. Johnson, *A Journey to the Western Islands of Scotland,* ed. Mary Lascelles (New Haven: Yale University Press, 1971), p. 26.

77. Burke, *Philosophical Inquiry,* p. 31.

78. See, for example, [Andrew Swinton or William Thomson], *Travels into Norway, Denmark and Russia* (London: G. G. J. and J. Robinson, 1792), p. vi.

79. Paterson, *Another Traveller!,* I, 153; [Johnson], *Literary Magazine* 1 (1756), 335; [Goldsmith], *MR* 17 (1757), 51; *CR* 4 (1757), 1. Concerning Johnson's attack on Hanway's discussion of tea in his *Journal,* see Boswell, *Life of Johnson,* I, 20, 309, 313-314; *The Journal of a Tour to the Hebrides, with Samuel Johnson, LL.D.* in Boswell's *Life of Johnson,* V, 23.

80. *CR* 4 (1757), 2; *MR* 17 (1757), 51; Jonas Hanway, *A Journal of Eight Days Journey from Portsmouth to Kingston upon Thames,* 2d ed. (London: H. Woodfall, 1757), I, 89, 211, 225. In contrast, Georg Forster's *Voyage round the World* (1777) receives critical praise for introducing its reflections in a careful and suitable fashion (see *CR* 43 [1777], 213).

81. *AR* 15 (1793), 376-377; *CR* 4 (1757), 2; Paterson, *Another Traveller!,* I, viii; *CR* 2d ser., 21 (1797), 256.

82. Brydone, *Tour,* I, 141; Boswell, *Life of Johnson,* II, 467-468; III, 356.

83. *CR* 30 (1770), 348; ibid., p. 194; Andrew Burnaby, *Burnaby's Travels through North America,* ed. Rufus Rockwell Wilson (New York: A. Wessels, 1904), pp. 24, 153-154. Also see *MR* 43 (1771), 222.

84. *CR* 21 (1766), 208.

85. See Brydone, *Tour,* I, 330-332.

86. Joseph Hucks, *A Pedestrian Tour through North Wales* (London: J. Debrett, 1795), pp. 28-29; John Hassell, *Tour of the Isle of Wight,* I, 112; William Gilpin, *Observations on the River Wye, and Several Parts of South Wales,* 5th ed. (London: T. Cadell junior, 1800), p. 47.

87. See Nichols, *Literary Anecdotes,* VIII, 657-658.

88. *The Complete Prose Works of Matthew Arnold,* ed. R. H. Super (Ann Arbor: University of Michigan Press, 1960-1977), IX, 202 [fonts reversed]. Also see my forthcoming article, "Samuel Ireland's Influence on Wordsworth's 'Tintern Abbey'."

89. Parks, "Turn to the Romantic," p. 24.

90. R. S. Crane, "Philosophy, Literature, and the History of Ideas," in *The Idea of the Humanities and Other Essays: Critical and Historical* (Chicago: University of Chicago Press, 1967), I, 187.

## CONCLUSION

1. James Boswell, *Life of Johnson,* ed. George Birkbeck Hill and L. F. Powell (Oxford: Clarendon Press, 1934-1950), IV, 186 n. 3; *Johnsonian Miscellanies,* ed. G. B. Hill (Oxford: Clarendon Press, 1897), II, 303.

2. Walter Scott, *The Life of John Dryden* (1834), ed. Bernard Kreissman (Lincoln: University of Nebraska Press, 1963), p. 395; Patrick Anderson, *Over the Alps: Reflections on Travel and Travel Writing* (London: Hart-Davis, 1969), p. 21. For a bibliography of recent arguments concerning Johnson's *Journey,* see Francis R. Hart, "Johnson as Philosophic Traveler: The Perfecting of an Idea," *ELH* 36 (1969), 679, n. 2.

3. Hermann Keyserling, *The Travel Diary of a Philosopher,* trans. J. Holroyd Reece (New York: Harcourt, 1925), I, 9.

4. Jeffrey Hart, "Johnson's *A Journey to the Western Islands:* History as Art," *EIC* 10 (1960), 44.

5. Samuel Johnson, *A Journey to the Western Islands of Scotland,* ed. Mary Lascelles (New Haven: Yale University Press, 1971), p. 164; Boswell, *The Journal of a Tour to the Hebrides, with Samuel Johnson, LL.D.,* in Boswell's *Life of Johnson,* V, 416.

6. See, for example, Edward Godfrey Cox, *A Reference Guide to the Literature of Travel* (Seattle: University of Washington Press, 1935-1949), III, 32, 40.

7. Alexander Gerard, "Appendix, concerning the Question, Whether Poetry Be Properly an Imitative Art," in *An Essay on Taste (1759), together with Observations concerning the Imitative Nature of Poetry,* intro. Walter J. Hipple, 3d ed. (1780; Gainesville, Fla.: Scholar's Facsimiles & Reprints, 1963), pp. 278, 282.

8. Lazzaro Spallanzani, *Travels in the Two Sicilies and Some Parts of the Appennines* (1798), cited in *CR* 2d ser., 22 (1798), 257.

9. Marjorie Hope Nicolson, *Mountain Gloom and Mountain Glory: The Development of the Aesthetics of the Infinite* (Ithaca: Cornell University Press, 1959), p. 306.

10. *British Critic* 4 (1794), 391; also see Charles François Olivier Rosette, Chevalier de Brucourt, *Essai sur l'éducation de la noblesse,* nouvelle ed. (Paris: Durand, 1748), II, 170-192.

# INDEX

156